MW01108032

BROADMAN

from TRAINING PaNTS To TRAINING WHEELS—

To Friendship International,

TONI SORTOR

from TRAINING PaNTS To TRAINING WHEELS—

Best wishes,

Josie Short

16820

FLEMING H. REVELL COMPANY
OLD TAPPAN, NEW JERSEY

Scripture quotations in this book are taken from the King James Version of the Bible.

Library of Congress Cataloging-in-Publication Data

Sortor, Toni, date
    From training pants to training wheels.

    1. Mothers—Prayer-books and devotions—
English.   2. Parents—Prayer-books and devotions—
English.   3. Mother and child.   4. Sortor, Toni,
date   . I. Title.
BV4529.S54 1988   649'.1   88-3236
ISBN 0-8007-1589-6

TO

Laura, Jim, and Steve.
I tried not to embarrass you, kids.

Contents

Introduction

This book is not designed to be a guide to child rearing; I'm not an expert on children. I have twenty-two years of experience as a mother, but that doesn't make me an expert. Grandmothers are experts.

This isn't supposed to be a serious book. I may occasionally sound flippant about a problem you're taking quite seriously. Believe me, I know how serious raising children can be! In the long run, however, it's more funny than serious.

When I speak of the generic child, I use *he* instead of *he or she*. *He* could apply to either sex most of the time, unless I'm talking about a child in big trouble. Then it's usually a boy.

The chapters are short for a reason. You can easily read one during "Sesame Street" and still have time to laugh at Big Bird now and then. I know you don't have a free hour to spend with a book; squeeze this in whenever you find a few free minutes. Enjoy.

from TRAINING PaNTS To TRAINING WHEELS—

1

Axioms:
Birth to One Year

Baby hair smells nice when it's clean; baby hair is seldom clean.

A mother's best friend is her pediatrician.

Try to remember when you feed beets to the baby. It saves a lot of panic the next day.

All little boys wet as soon as the diaper comes off.

No illness becomes serious until the pediatrician's office closes.

Babies look exactly like whichever side of the family is visiting.

Most little boys have beautiful heads of hair; most little girls look like Telly Savalas.

Nothing is as slippery as a tiny baby in the bath.

2

Pregnancy

There is absolutely nothing funny about being pregnant.

The whole process is hysterical.

That's a paradox. That's pregnancy.

I spent 826.7 days of my life in the state of pregnancy. (If you want to check my math, allow for three children, one of whom was two weeks late. Also figure on 4.3 weeks in a month. Take my word for it.) If it hadn't been such an investment of time and energy, I'd prefer to forget all 826.7 days. Some of them were wonderful. Some were awful. I wouldn't want to relive any of them.

Some doctor of the male persuasion said pregnancy is a self-inflicted, self-limiting condition. Whoever he is, I hope his mother knows he's talking like that. I hope his wife made him pay!

I personally enjoyed being pregnant—on the six or seven days I felt well. Most of the time I was hungry, sick, uncomfortable, and without a stitch of clothing that fit me or any occasion.

But I had a secret. I knew something no one else did,

not even my husband. (From an occasional look on her face, I had a sneaking suspicion my mother might know the secret, but certainly no one else did.) God and I were building ourselves a miracle—quietly, privately, in secret places, in secret ways. For the first time in my life, I *knew* how babies were made!

A man reading that sentence won't understand it, and neither will a woman who's never been pregnant. It's unexplainable but real. Ask your mother about it.

In the meantime relish your pregnancy. Enjoy the secret. And, most importantly, remember that having a baby is worth every second of those nine long months.

Lord, thank You for sharing the miracle of pregnancy with me each day as the child within me grows. Although I don't know him yet—What color are his eyes? Will he be short like the rest of us, or tall and lean?—in a very real way I know him as I know no other. Keep him safe and warm, please, and help me keep my sense of humor and perspective in the months and years to come.

Strength and honour are her clothing; and she shall rejoice in time to come.

Proverbs 31:25

3

B ill?"

"Mpf?"

"Wake up. I think I'm in labor."

"Huhn. How do you know?"

"Someone's sitting on my stomach."

"Fool dog! Where is he?"

"No. No dog. It's labor."

"Hurt?"

"Not yet. One's starting now. Time it for me."

"I can't see my watch. Where is it?"

"Turn on the light!"

"It's two-thirty-two in the morning. Should I call the doctor?"

Husbands always want to call the doctor. They also want to drive you to the hospital at breakneck speed, running red lights and maybe picking up a police escort, if they're lucky. It's rarely necessary.

My children took a day or two to make up their minds about being born. We're a cautious family, so I figure the ride to the hospital convinced them to stay put for a while until things calmed down.

Checking into a hospital is always interesting. They lower you into a wheelchair with much concern, balance your suitcase on the small amount of lap still available, and let you sit alone in the hall for the next forty-five minutes while your husband proves he can afford this baby. I often wondered what they'd do if he forgot his Blue Cross card.

Eventually you will be proven worthy and wheeled up to maternity. There you are given a wonderful gift: You are allowed to use the bathroom. Forty-five minutes in the hall make this your *first* priority. After that, you might as well hang up a few pictures and dust under the bed; this room is going to be your home for quite a while.

Although I had my children before husbands were considered necessary to the process, my husband was allowed to stay with me in the labor room and doze off in a straight-backed chair until things began to get serious. Then all concerned would send him home and this child and I would buckle down to work. The waiting was over for us all, which was a relief, but it was a relief tinged with a good bit of nervousness and apprehension.

Finally, Lord! After all these months, we're finally going to produce something. We're going to answer all those questions about blue eyes or brown, big ears or small, girl or boy. Is it too late to change my mind about this whole thing? Can I call it off now and go home? Just thought I'd ask. Okay, let's get on with it. Hold my hand, Lord?

To every thing there is a season, and a time to every purpose under the heaven: A time to be born. . . .

Ecclesiastes 3:1, 2

Taxi! 19

4

Birth

Now we're getting into the heavy stuff. Birth is so serious, so momentous; how can anyone be flippant about it? It's probably the drugs.

Nowadays women are refusing anesthesia, and their husbands are staying with them through it all to be part of the experience. More power to them, but I'm glad I had my babies back in the unenlightened ages!

My husband would have loved to have seen his children born. He's like that—kind, concerned, willing to do his share. But let's be honest: How much could he really *do* for me at that point? When it got down to the sweating and grunting, what earthly good was he?

So I sent him home. I liked the guy, and it hurt me to watch him hurt for me. (I also had some, but not much, self-respect still left. I say the most terrible things under painkillers.) My husband went back to painting the bathroom ceiling, and I, wanting to get my job over and done with, said something like, "Yo, Demerol! Over here!"

In no time at all I woke up in a sunny room and found people smiling at me. My first reaction was to pat my stomach. Yup, more or less flat. Look, my feet were visible! And I hurt in places no one ever wants to hurt.

Then, in my happy but semiconscious state, I heard my husband say that yes, I'd had the baby, he was fine, and what should we name him?

From Training Pants to Training Wheels

Name him? I hadn't even *seen* him yet! Why did I have to name him now? He wasn't going to be signing any checks, was he? But as it seemed important to everyone, we named him. I never believed in figuring out names in advance. If I had my way, we wouldn't name children until they hit eighteen and we would know if they're a Poindexter or a Rambo. But the grandparents were on the phone lobbying for some family name and a decision had to be made now. As a result all three of our kids have plain first names, ones given more or less off the top of my fuzzy head. The middle names were up to my husband and the assembled relatives. Don't ask one of my kids what his middle name is!

Eventually all the well-wishers left and a nurse trundled in a blue blanket, which she deposited in my arms, and left me to count toes. Which I did. Doesn't everyone?

The first look at a new baby is rather like viewing an original Dali. Everything seems to be a little out of place, but, Lord, it's beautiful!

"So *you're* the little fellow who's been kicking in time to the stereo all these months? You've got a black eye, you know? And your father's tiny ears. How are you doing, Jim? Yeah, you're a Jim, all right. Welcome to the world, my little secret."

> *Father of us all, I'm no saint, yet today I rejoice in the honor of motherhood. If I could carry a tune, I would sing for joy on my bed, too. Truth is, I'm more or less speechless today! How did I ever do this—create a totally new life, a new soul? It took three of us to do it, I know that much. And I'm sure it'll take all three of us to raise this little miracle. Thank You for my son, Lord, from the bottom of my heart.*

Let the saints be joyful in glory: let them sing aloud upon
their beds.

Psalms 149:5

5 Hospitals

I was in no hurry to take my baby home. He'd kept me
in labor for three days; he could wait for me. It was
peaceful and friendly in the hospital. People kept sending
me flowers and dropping by to chat. I was so *tired*.

Right after the naming ceremony, I had to make another
decision—breast or bottle? I had one day to decide, so I
looked around to see who was doing what. What I
discovered was that mothers who breastfeed get woken
up for the 6:00 A.M. feeding, while bottle mothers are free
until 10:00 A.M. I *told* you I was tired. I chose the bottle.

The baby trundle was a unique feature of the maternity
ward in my day (everything's different now, better). You
would be visiting quietly with your husband when the
rumble started, a noise similar to a bulldozer working two
blocks away. Suddenly the doors at the end of the hall
would be thrown open and a phalanx of nurses would
sweep down the hall yelling, "Babies on the ward! All

From Training Pants to Training Wheels

visitors *out!*" Those visitors who dawdled were in for it. My husband still shivers at the sound of little wheels on linoleum.

A nurse wheeled in a plastic bassinet with a blue bow, checked my wrist tag against the baby's, and deposited one baby and one bottle in my arms. Then she did something I could never get used to—she left! I wanted to shout, "Wait! What do I do now?" But you can't look that stupid, so I put the two things she left me together and the baby sucked away. I'm glad he knew what to do.

Babies are amazing little eaters. They can't do one single thing for themselves except eat. Mine was a champion eater. He'd lie there in my arms, bundled in layers of blankets, and suck away like a little worker. Imagine cheeks and tiny lips pumping away, eyes closed tightly, fists curled, and sweat breaking out on his little forehead. Amazing! From day one, he never sent an uneaten ounce back to the nursery.

He burped good, too. Maybe it had something to do with the jolt he got as I tried to get him to my shoulder without breaking him. I'd protect the back of his head from drooping, only to have his forehead crash against my shoulder. Not enough hands. I kept him there once he was set, because I couldn't figure out how to get him back down. Eventually a nurse rescued us both and trundled the baby away.

After five days of rest and glory punctuated by visits from a hungry, warm, dry baby, they kicked me out. Even though I still felt like a wet dishrag and had never changed one diaper or been woken up once for a two o'clock feeding, they packed me up, handed me my baby, and sent me home. I was not ready for that!

Father of all mothers, what have they done? They've let me loose with this baby I barely know. I'm not qualified for this! And my husband, willing as he is, is more frightened than I. Well, if this is the way it's supposed to be, I'll have to assume You and the hospital know what You're doing. But please stay close for a while, will You? Really close!

Teach me good judgment and knowledge: for I have believed thy commandments.

Psalms 119:66

6

Going Home

Once you get used to the idea of leaving the hospital, the day you bring home a new baby becomes the best day of your life. Finally, he's yours. Someone said you could keep him; no nurse can whisk him off anymore. It's the ultimate Christmas present.

Even the world looks nicer on the way home. Not everyone is wearing hospital whites, for one thing. There are flowers growing in dirt, where they belong, not dying

From Training Pants to Training Wheels

in vases. And your mother is waiting at home with your favorite meal. Life isn't half bad.

It takes about half an hour for reality to hit. The baby soon tires of being passed from relative to relative and will either begin to scream or wet Grandpa's best suit (or do both). In no time superfluous relatives will disappear and you'll have to send out your husband for something vital like disposable diapers or formula. Until he returns, you and Grandma are stuck with a pathetically crying baby.

No nurse is going to waft in and take care of this kid! If he never stops crying (and it sounds like he might not), *you'll* be responsible. If the formula gives him gas, you're the one who will walk him all night. If the dog licks his face and gives him a horrid disease, it's your fault. This is not a doll you're playing with—this is one huge, lifelong responsibility. And you don't feel all that well, either.

If you're lucky, your mother will see the panic on your face, recognize it for what it is, and send you to bed while she copes. There's about a fifty-fifty chance of that.

Listen: You'll live and so will the baby. Eventually you'll find the switch that turns him off for four hours. Then you can begin to worry about why he's sleeping so long! Welcome home. You've done a good thing; now lean on the Lord. He'll give you all the help you need.

Dear Lord, this baby frightens me! There are so many ways he could be hurt, and I know so little about babies. I worry when he cries; I worry when he doesn't; and I worry about all the things that I don't know enough to worry about yet. They say this will pass and I'll grow more confident with each day. Until then, Lord, be my strength. Contain my fears and magnify my joy, for all our sakes.

Going Home

The Lord is my light and my salvation; whom shall I fear? the Lord is the strength of my life; of whom shall I be afraid?

Psalms 27:1

7

2:00 A.M.

___

You're supposed to be happy with a new baby, and much of the time you are. You've survived the pregnancy with your marriage more or less intact. You've even survived three to five days of hospital food. Now you and the baby can get on with enjoying each other.

But how do you enjoy someone who wakes you up every four hours screaming? It's not bad at first. Maybe your husband helps out by getting the baby up, changing him, and warming the bottle. All you have to do is the feeding, rechanging (yes, they get *very* wet in that twenty minutes), and rebedding.

Note: If your husband does his part here, you will pay for it forever. For the rest of your life he will claim to the grandchildren that *he* totally took care of the 2:00 A.M.

feeding. Those who breastfeed may possibly have a re-joinder here, but don't count on it.

This feeding is simplified if you breastfeed. It saves a few dark, cold trips to the refrigerator, when the chances are best that you will stumble on the stairs and experience great pain from tender stitches. You are, after all, sleep-deprived and not physically 100 percent well.

Babies are adorable at 2:00 A.M. They're warm and cuddly on a cold night. They look deeply into your eyes and make you happy to be shivering while you wait for the burp. They also spit up a lot on your pillow.

I would suggest you feed your baby in your bed, unless you're one of those people who wakes up in a flash. I was incoherent at 2:00 A.M. and found it comforting to know that if I fell asleep with the baby in my arms, he would fall onto a nice soft bed. It happened. It didn't hurt any of us, and he was right handy when his 6:00 A.M. feeding rolled around.

Two o'clock feedings go on forever, night after night, with no weekends or sick days off. You're never totally rested. You fall asleep in front of the TV at 7:00 P.M. as your husband tells you about his day. You nod off when your in-laws come to admire their son's baby. You doze on line in the supermarket.

But one fine day the pediatrician says the magic words, "Let's try him on a little cereal." In a matter of a few nights, your wake-up call doesn't come until three or four in the morning. Then one day you wake up in a panic at 6:00 A.M. and realize you've been asleep since 10:00 P.M. You're rested! Where's the baby?

You rush into the nursery expecting the worst, only to find your heir peering at you with his big fawn eyes, a look of wonder on his face. Even *he's* surprised. Two o'clock feedings have been cancelled.

This is one of the most physically taxing times of your life, but it's also one of the happiest. Accept all the help you're offered, sleep whenever you can, and enjoy the warmth of holding your baby in the still of the night.

Lord, I didn't know I could be so tired and so happy at the same time. Somehow You're giving me the strength to go on with much too little in the way of real rest. I'll make it, with Your help. Thank You for these late-night opportunities to hold my baby close and share this closeness with him. It's so nice to see a happy face—at any hour!

The Lord will give strength unto his people; the Lord will bless his people with peace.

Psalms 29:11

8 Baby Watching

Baby watching is one of life's sublime pleasures. It serves no logical purpose, but even the most organized parents enjoy it.

You begin to watch a newborn baby sleep out of nervousness: Is he still breathing? How can he just lie there and sleep like that for hours on end? Even before he wakes up his little mouth twitches, puckers up, makes little sucking motions. His arms get stuck under his body now and then, but he doesn't seem to care. Little beads of sweat are visible among the sparse hairs on his head. Maybe the blanket should come off. You know you should grab a nap before he wakes up again, but you put your finger into his tiny fist and feel it grasped in sleep. It's a good thing you're home alone because you must look foolish bending over a sleeping baby.

As he grows a little older, his body parts begin to function more like a real person's. One time he'll be stretched out on his face, snoring softly with one arm dangling out of the crib. The next time, he'll be curled up at the top of the crib, his hand mashing his nose in an unconscious attempt to plug a finger into his mouth. Occasionally he'll sigh or whimper, twitching his face into an obviously unhappy expression. Gas? Hunger? Do babies have bad dreams?

He's beginning to make larger body movements now, kicking off his blanket in his sleep, getting his finger into his mouth with ease. You find him balanced on his side one day. The next day he'll surprise both you and himself by waking on his back and scream in outrage when he can't get back to his stomach. Even at this young age he knows he's a stomach sleeper. You'll roll him over and he'll fall into an exhausted slumber. You'll do this several times a day until he develops the muscles to do it for himself.

One day you'll hear the crib rocking in the silent house.

Now what? Somehow he has gotten his knees up under his body and is lifting his fanny in the air and pushing his head up against the crib. He's sound asleep, rocking back and forth to the same rhythm you used to put him asleep in the rocking chair, a real smile on his face.

Babies grow in their sleep. They flex their muscles and gain control of their bodies right before your eyes, with no effort whatsoever on your part. Watching a baby sleep is watching a miracle happen.

So much is going on in his little life, Lord, right before my eyes. I don't understand how these changes are taking place, but I'm certainly enjoying watching them. Thank You for this wonder You've entrusted to my care.

I will praise thee; for I am fearfully and wonderfully made: marvellous are thy works; and that my soul knoweth right well.

Psalms 139:14

9

Diapers

This is a potentially disgusting chapter, but I'll try to be discreet. The thing is, you really do have to know about diapers; they'll be a major factor in your life for some years to come.

Would you believe they hadn't invented disposable diapers when my first child was born? They had, thank heaven, invented the diaper service. Being a sensible person, I called the service as soon as I learned I was pregnant, in case there was a waiting list. There wasn't, and the diaper pail arrived with a pile of clean diapers the day before we brought our daughter home from the hospital.

I loved my diaper-service man. He arrived on time twice a week and walked off with what could have been one of my biggest problems, all for four dollars a week. He checked on our daughter's progress at each visit, passed on helpful hints, and, most importantly, gave me an adult to talk to twice a week. Those of you who have never met a diaper-service man have missed out on something.

By the time my second child came along, so had disposable diapers. But they were new, and as there was some stigma attached to them in my mind, I stuck with the diaper-service man (who cheerfully doubled my order and told me how bad disposable diapers were for a baby's tender bottom). I did, however, use disposables when they were more convenient than cloth diapers. That's any time you plan to be out in public for more than one hour. I've traveled with cloth diapers and I've traveled with disposables and disposables are far better. (One exception: We never made it through customs as fast as the time we returned from an island with a suitcase full of carefully packaged but dirty cloth diapers!)

Child number three never felt cloth on his tender bottom. By then disposables actually worked, with minimum leakage. I say minimum because little boys can find their way around *any* diaper ever made. Still, if I had it to do over again today (bite your tongue, as my mother-in-law used to say), I'd go the disposable route all the way.

Once that decision is made, you're faced with another that no one ever seems to mention. You begin to think you're the only mother in the world who doesn't know the answer to a vital question: How often is a baby supposed to be changed? It doesn't take you long to figure out that it's impossible to keep a baby 100 percent dry. But where's the break-even point?

Well, it would be pretty stupid to wake up a sleeping baby just to change his diaper, so that rules out a lot of times. When he wakes up, it will be obvious that he needs changing. When he's ready to go back to sleep, it never hurts to do it again. For the first few months, the problem sort of takes care of itself that way.

But soon the baby will start staying awake for some social interaction, and getting-up and going-to-bed changes won't be enough. I always took my hint from my husband or visitors: When anyone picked up my baby and said "Ugh!" it was time for a change. Anytime a rash appeared, it was time to be a little more conscientious. Nature has a way of providing plenty of hints in these matters.

It's not going to be too long before your baby starts telling you when he needs to be changed. One day he's going to walk up to you, as my first son did, look you firmly in the eye, and say, "Change me, Mommy." Since I'd just changed him five minutes before, I said no. At which point he walked himself over to a corner, made a face, smiled, walked back, looked me in the eye, and said, "*Now* change me, Mommy!" I changed him—and bought him a potty. But that's another story.

The point is, there's lots of help available—be it common sense, from books, from other mothers, or from your child himself. You're not in this alone.

It's so hard to know what to do and what not to do, Lord, but thank You for Nature's help along the way. Sometimes my baby seems to know more about raising children than I do. We're learning from each other, growing together each day.

So is the kingdom of God, as if a man should cast seed into the ground; And should sleep, and rise night and day, and the seed should spring and grow up, he knoweth not how. For the earth bringeth forth fruit of herself; first the blade, then the ear, after that the full corn in the ear.

Mark 4:26–28

10

I don't know if anyone's ever pointed this out to you, but babies eat a lot. Even without cereal and fruit, a baby will soon be draining six bottles a day at eight ounces per bottle, or forty-eight ounces a day. That's three pounds of food a day for a baby that weighs ten pounds at best. And even then you get the feeling he could down more, if he were awake more often. Where's he putting it all?

Every baby book you read will tell you something different about feeding babies. As far as I recall they can't digest much, but they're apt to try. My babies even thought my glasses were appetizing. One of them spent a year trying to catch the cat; when she finally did, the fur turned her off her victory meal. Another lived on rug fuzz until he learned to walk. (I suspect he still enjoys it now and then.)

I was sort of relaxed about feeding my babies. I figured they knew what their bodies needed, so if one spat puréed liver at me, we scrapped the liver. The kid had good sense.

I wasn't as liberal with the first baby, of course. She was raised by the book and her pediatrician. If they agreed it was time to add egg yolk to her cereal, she got egg yolk. All in all, she came out okay. She lived on her own all through college and actually cooked vegetables. She still hates egg yolks, though.

34   From Training Pants to Training Wheels

New parents do have a tendency to think every meal is vital. One mistake and the baby could get a rash. If he doesn't eat his strained peas once, he'll grow up short. There are parents who skip two meals a day and live at fast-food restaurants but have a fit if Junior dozes off and leaves two ounces of formula in his bottle.

Relax a little and enjoy feeding the baby. It's probably the most meaningful event in his life. He gets a kick out of watching Mommy open her mouth wide as she moves the spoon toward him. He chortles when Daddy makes a fool out of himself by playing airplane. He *loves* it when the cat shares his strained liver.

Do watch out for daddies, though. They believe babies have no discrimination and tend to mix apricots and beef into one disgusting spoonful. Then they laugh at the baby's face, mix up another portion, and call you in to watch. You have to protect the baby at times like these. You also have to be sure the baby gets his fair share. My husband used to hog the cream cheese dessert if the baby's attention wandered and I was out of the room. I preferred peaches, myself.

In short, enjoy feeding your baby. All too soon he'll be ordering pizza for breakfast!

Lord, this baby certainly loves to eat! I can almost see the food turning into good bones and muscles as I feed him. Mealtimes are special for all of us, but there's nothing like the joy my baby experiences as I feed him, and the pleasure it gives to me. Thank You for providing for us in ways both physical and spiritual.

These wait all upon thee; and thou mayest give them their meat in due season. That thou givest them they gather: thou openest thine hand, they are filled with good.

Psalms 104:27, 28

11

Oops!

Some babies have iron stomachs. They can swap their zwieback for the puppy's biscuit and experience no ill effects whatsoever. I never had such a baby. Mine spent their first years swaddled in bibs or with clean diapers draped around their chests.

Spitting up doesn't bother a baby in the least. He doesn't do the laundry. It's not his three-piece suit that has to go to the dry cleaner twice in one week. He couldn't care less if he spits on his baptismal gown in front of the whole congregation (and he will). Most babies are capable of cooing, gurgling, smiling, and ruining your sofa, all at the same time.

You have to check with the pediatrician, but chances are you will be told everything's fine, don't worry, he'll grow out of it. The doctor, who is certainly no fool, will tell you this while standing a safe distance from your baby.

You do not have this option. If your baby erupts every time he's jiggled, you're still going to cuddle him, pat his back, and toss him onto your shoulder without remembering to put a diaper in front of him first. In about two weeks every piece of clothing you own is going to be permanently stained. That's okay, because you need a new wardrobe as you lose your "baby fat," anyway.

Grandparents have two possible reactions to a spitting

grandchild. They may be convinced you're totally mismanaging his diet and endangering his health (your husband's parents usually fall into this category). Or they may smile calmly as you mop them off and pronounce their grandchild obviously well fed and happy (your parents). Either way, Grandpa will never again wear his Harris tweed jacket to your house!

This does not go on forever, no matter how it seems now. As soon as the baby begins to assume a more vertical position, the spitting eases up. By the time he's sitting up or standing on his own, gravity takes hold and your problems are over. Until then, don't plan on getting dressed to go out before the baby-sitter arrives.

Everything good in life costs something, and this is a small price to pay for the joy of having a baby in the house.

Lord, as long as I know he's healthy, I'm more than happy to have him around to clean up after.

The Lord recompense thy work, and a full reward be given thee of the Lord God of Israel, under whose wings thou art come to trust.

Ruth 2:12

12

No church nursery is ever far enough from the sanctuary. Not that crying babies have ever disturbed me—unless they were my own.

Like every other young mother in church, I could distinguish my baby's wail from that of the other wailers. We parents of nursery children all sat in the back rows so we could make our exits without disturbing anyone; some Sundays we just stood at the back of the church, knowing it was not going to be a good day. I don't think I heard one complete sermon in five years. The organist would crank it up for the offering hymn and all the babies would go off in a rising crescendo that emptied the back pews.

Finally I gave up and volunteered to supervise the nursery. It was easier to be in there with them than listen to them. Besides, it was interesting to see how long an individual mother could hold out. Would Mrs. B make it to the Gospel reading this week? Would Mrs. F *ever* come in and claim her inconsolate daughter? Would Mr. G come in, yell at his toddler, and leave us to calm his weeping son again? How firm could we be with the minister's hair-pulling daughter, who was the only child guaranteed to be with us until the end of the service?

It was useless to hope for a quiet hour or napping babies as the parental parade kept the kids in a constant state of expectation. Surely if they yelled loud enough, their particular parent would magically appear. Once the opening ebb and flow quieted down and the processional had echoed away we'd have a few minutes of peace, but soon the organ would shake the toy box again. A slight respite occurred during the sermon, then we were into the recessional and full-scale nursery revolution. They were hungry, bored, and sleepy. They wanted to go home *now!*

When it finally dawned on me that no one in our family was getting anything out of the service, we did the sensible thing: We hired a sitter to stay home with the kids and we went to church on our own. After that, I never heard the babies in the nursery.

No one ever said children were easy, did they, Lord? They change all aspects of my life. I'm constantly adjusting my schedule and refitting my life to theirs. But that's okay. That's what being a family is all about.

O come, let us sing unto the Lord: let us make a joyful noise to the rock of our salvation. Let us come before his presence with thanksgiving, and make a joyful noise unto him with psalms.

Psalms 95:1, 2

13

Axioms:
One to Two Years

At any dinner table the dog sits under the youngest child.

A child perfectly capable of feeding himself hot dogs becomes incapable of feeding himself as soon as spinach is put on his plate.

Consider yourself blessed if your child's first word is fit for Grandma's ears.

Babies get too tired to walk as soon as your hands are full.

Your baby gets his free spirit from your husband. His stubbornness comes from *your* side of the family.

To your baby, food from your plate tastes better than the same food on his plate.

Every baby knows toys belong on the floor outside the playpen.

14

One

I have a theory that the odd years in a child's life are fun, but watch out for those even numbers. One is nice. You've all survived tiny babyhood and spitting up, and it's fairly safe to take a one-year-old out in public. It's not easy, but it is possible.

Babies at one year now fit into a car seat without looking like their backs will suffer permanent damage or they will slide through the straps and slip quietly onto the floor. Their attention span is short, but any good mother can keep up a babble of distracting talk as far as the supermarket.

"Oh, look at the birdie, Laura. See the birdie?"

"Bid?"

"B-i-r-d. Over there. By the nice lady." The one that's wondering why you're pointing at her.

"Gamma?"

"No, that's not Grandma. Grandma has red hair, re-member?"

" 'member?"

"Re-mem-ber. Do you remember Grandma?"

From Training Pants to Training Wheels

"Gamma! Gamma!" This is screamed at the top of her lungs as you pull away from the little old lady and leave her on the corner.

"There's the store, Laura. We'll go buy you some baby food, okay?"

" 'ot dogs!"

"Junior beef."

"Pud'n!"

"What? Pudding? All right. And junior beef."

" 'ot dogs!"

You'll have to carry on the rest of this conversation without me. I've done it too often, and I always bought the 'ot dogs and pud'n.

I miss those mobile conversations with a one-year-old. Even now, when we're all traveling together, I find myself saying, "Oh, look, a cow!" As if none of the teens crammed into the backseat had ever seen a cow.

One-year-olds are infinitely interesting. They're visibly becoming people. Maybe not the people you had hoped they would be, but people nevertheless. They learn how to walk and absolutely refuse to stay in the playpen, so they're a wonderful source of exercise. Tell a one-year-old to come to you and he'll run the other way with a maniacal laugh. They love simple pleasures: chasing the dog around the table, pulling everything off the table, eating everything they pulled off the table, falling and cracking their heads on the table.

During this year a baby will learn the meaning of the word *no*. He'd better, or he'll never make it through another year. It usually happens in the kitchen when he reaches for a hot burner or pot. Hearing you scream "NO!" like a madwoman and being summarily pulled away from something tends to leave an impression. That kind of *no* they remember and respect.

But there are other forms of *no* that get no respect. Pushing the neighbor's baby flat on his rear end gets a swift *no*. Unfortunately, the little kid probably deserved the push and your mental equivocation will instantly be recognized by your child. Soon he'll only push when you're not looking. You have to keep trying to socialize him, but don't expect a lot of success.

Concentrate on the lifesaving *nos* during this year; there are enough of them to keep you busy. The less serious infractions can be dealt with through physical restraint (use it now, it doesn't work for long) or through simplified reasoning.

"No, Laura. Don't pull the cat's tail. It hurts her."

"Hurts?"

"Yes. You see. . . ." It's never necessary to finish this sentence. Cats don't recognize the word *no* as valid.

"Waaa!"

"See? You hurt the cat, so she hurt you." Then you physically restrain the baby or it's curtains for the cat.

One is fun. Enjoy it, because two is just around the corner.

Lord, I'm not exacty sure what's going on inside my baby's head these days, but it must be busy in there! He's like a little learning machine, sucking up new skills right and left with little discrimination. Keeping him safe and happy requires all my energy and time. I feel myself becoming impatient, trapped, and lonely. When I feel like that, Lord, remind me of the good times the two of us have every day and the joy he brings in his tiny, reaching hands.

From Training Pants to Training Wheels

Search me, O God, and know my heart: try me, and know my thoughts.

Psalms 139:23

15

Words

I had one early talker, a normal one, and a late one. The early talker was lots of fun until I realized she was never going to shut up. The late talker had us worried until we realized there was nothing wrong with a child who could take apart—and rebuild properly—every toy in the house.

I thought the "vocalizing" stage was the most fun. My neighbor calls it talking Chinese. (He's German, so his kids "talked" in three languages—German, English, and Chinese.) There's nothing more adorable than a baby holding his empty bottle and seriously giving it what-for in vowels and consonants. The words aren't there, but there's no doubt about his meaning.

My early talker talked in self-defense. She was the only child at that point, so we went everywhere together and I talked to her for company. When she was nine months old, she said her first word, a grouping of three syllables. Her second word was *remember*.

Her first word? Well, you'll have to use your imagination. She had just crawled to the top of the stairs on her hands and knees for the very first time. Those were thirteen very high, very hard steps. Then her hand slipped and she knocked her chin on the top step. Suffice it to say it was a clear word, suitable to the occasion, and I couldn't tell it to my mother-in-law. (My mother laughed herself silly.) After that word and *remember*, she got around to *Mommy* and *Daddy*.

Our late talker's first word was *truck*. He said it just before he hit the neighbors' boy over the head with one, so maybe it was really *duck*, but I think we heard him right. He followed that with *dog* before he got to us. His priorities are still pretty much the same eighteen years later.

Our on-schedule child said *Daddy* first, then got around to me when I took away his hot dogs. His vocabulary expanded the most rapidly of all, since he had a big brother and sister to teach him. Besides, he needed words to summon help quite often.

You see your child differently once he's talking. Before, you wonder if anything is going on in there. His world and yours only really touch on the physical levels of food, discomfort, and diapers. You wonder if he has a sense of humor. Does he ever wonder where Daddy goes all day? Does he know he's not the same kind of animal as the dog he crawls around with all day? What's soaking in, and what isn't?

Then the words begin and all your questions are answered. Our daughter laughed after she said her first word. At nine months she knew it was a bad word and thought it was funny. Our son wondered where Daddy went and soon learned "Take me!" with outstretched arms. Our other son knew he wasn't a dog and a dog wasn't a horsey. Daddy was a horsey and gave rides after dinner.

Suddenly the world was open to them, and because we fed and housed them, they were willing to share its wonder with us through their words. To see the world through the eyes of a one-year-old is to feel alive again.

Creator of all the wonder in my child's world, thank You for giving him the power of speech and the desire to share his joy with us. Thank You for letting us see the beauty of a dandelion through his eyes and for giving us this new and wonderful way to communicate with each other.

Sing unto him, sing psalms unto him: talk ye of all his wondrous works.

Psalms 105:2

16 Baby-Sitters

Eventually you're going to have to go out without your baby. Even though they're extremely portable, babies don't dress well enough for a formal dinner dance.

It's amazing how long you can go without hiring a baby-sitter. Now that so many women are working, food stores and doctors' offices are open past 5:00 P.M. Family members and neighbors don't mind you bringing along the baby for an evening of cards and conversation. It's even possible to shop for clothes or get the oil changed with a baby in tow.

But when your husband's boss invites you over for dinner, it's time to start looking for a responsible baby-sitter. Most new parents start the search within their extended family. If grandparents live close and show any inclination to do the job, grab them. They're a little rusty, but they love your child as much as you. If Aunt Madge ever says, "Anytime you need me, just call," call. Some lucky parents find a permanent answer to the baby-sitter problem right under their noses and are set for years.

Most do not. After doing the job once or twice, Aunt Madge, who never volunteers for anything, will suddenly become president of the League of Women Voters and be tied up with lots of evening and weekend meetings (since she became president). Grandpa's back will go out semi-permanently, or he and Grandma will pack up and move to Florida.

So what do you do when you run out of relatives? You start courting all the teenage girls in town. If you're smart, you'll make friends with the preteenagers, too; they grow up fast, and you'll need a sitter for the next thirteen years.

Baby-sitters have a short shelf life. They become usable around thirteen and by sixteen they are either dating or working, so you have to grab them young and pay them well. A well-stocked icebox, cable TV, and a baby that sleeps soundly are extremely desirable fringe benefits. If

From Training Pants to Training Wheels

you find a good one, offer her a permanent Saturday-night job, even if you don't always have somewhere to go and have to drive around town for two hours.

The hardest thing to do, once you find and train a sitter, is stay off the telephone. First, the line will be busy whenever you call. If it's not, no one will answer. Worse yet, a boy will answer. Either way you're going to drag your husband out of the restaurant before dessert and make him drive you home. There is no such thing as a "romantic weekend" away from home if your room has a direct-dial phone or you have a hidden cache of quarters in your purse. I'd get that distracted, jumpy look and my husband would immediately start looking for our waiter while wolfing down the last of his steak. He'd order dessert while I looked for a quarter and have the bill paid before I got back. Husbands learn fast.

When our children evolved into toddlers, we made a neighborhood pact and took care of one another's children when someone had to get away or be peeled off the wall. It worked out beautifully. The kids got to play with their best friends day and night for a whole weekend and destroy a different home every year. It wasn't all that bad when our turn came. We'd just stuff a few extra bodies into the bathtub with our kids and stock up on hot dogs and chocolate pudding mix.

Eventually your family will mature to the point where you will have an older child to leave as a sitter. Think about it. Do you really want to leave your only son and male heir with his older sister on the day he flushed her new shoes down the toilet?

Eventually you won't need a sitter at all. They will all be perfectly capable of calling their friends in for a party as soon as your car's taillights fade out of sight. But that's another story. For now, find yourself a sitter you can trust, treat yourself to some time off, and trust the Lord for the rest.

It's so hard to leave him with a sitter, Lord, but I do need some time for myself. Time to be alone with my husband, wander leisurely through a store, or just relax and collect myself. Watch over both my child and his sitter while I'm gone; let my mind be at ease until I return.

His soul shall dwell at ease; and his seed shall inherit the earth.

Psalms 25:13

17

Pets

If you're just beginning your family, now is the time to heed a warning: Don't adopt a pet. It's tempting when your baby is young to buy a puppy or kitten. You have Norman Rockwell visions of your son romping through a field with his faithful dog at his heels. The sun is shining,

From Training Pants to Training Wheels

the dog is fetching sticks, your son is laughing. It's a lie.

First, how far would you have to drive just to find a field? Second, who's going to teach the dog to fetch? Third, who's going to clean up your son when he romps through a cow pie?

Maybe your vision includes a kitten, a roaring fire, and your daughter laughing at the kitten as it plays with a piece of string. Is the kitten eating the string, clawing apart your daughter's new bedspread, and roasting its fleas by the fireplace?

The simple fact is parents of young children have too much to do without pets. Once your child has a pet, he *always* has a pet; one pet leaves, another comes along. It becomes a family tradition that cannot be broken until your children move out of the house and buy their own pets. So if you're now petless, think before you commit yourself to twenty years of canine (or feline) coexistence.

Most children under five don't even ask for pets, if you don't broach the subject. They keep busy without them or play with their friends' pets. Kids are traditionalists, and "We've never had pets" is a tradition they can respect. (This doesn't last. Children between the ages of eight and twelve will campaign actively for a pet. Enjoy it while you can.)

You also have to consider safety. Children under five are not safe playmates for puppies and kittens. They bite, kick, scratch, and tease (the kids, not the pets). You will spend half your life protecting your child from the world and your pets from your child. In the process you all become grumpy, and who wants to live with a grumpy cat?

Did I live by my own advice? Heck, no! We had a

grumpy cat by the time our first child was one. Before our second child was two, we had a grumpy cat and a frantic dog. By the time our third child was three, we had two grumpy cats, two frantic dogs, and twenty-three dying guppies. We now have one hostile cat, one paranoid dog, and one stir-crazy rabbit. See what happens when you buy that first puppy?

Some of us love little animals of all kinds, Lord. We rescue baby robins and cry when kamikaze squirrels run under our car wheels. We spend as much money on the vet as on the pediatrician. Life is precious to us in all its forms. Thank You for this gift.

Yea, the sparrow hath found an house, and the swallow a nest for herself, where she may lay her young, even thine altars, O Lord of hosts, my King, and my God.

Psalms 84:3

18

Babies are a lot of wonderful things; they are also dirty little beings. It's something mothers get used to with time. Fathers don't do as well. That's a generic statement, because my husband coped far better than I did. But since he escaped for eight hours every day I still claim my medal on the basis of effort alone.

A messy baby is to be expected. Sometimes it's even cute. All parents have pictures of their one-year-old covered ear to ear with birthday cake. No one really expects a dry baby at 2:00 A.M., although it might be nice of the fellow to try.

The thing to remember is that it doesn't get any better for a long time. The kind of dirt changes, but you can't expect a child to look or smell good on his own until puberty knocks him over the head.

There's nothing like a crawling baby as an indicator of when the rug needs vacuuming. In an emergency you can dress one in a fuzzy sleeper, let him loose on the kitchen floor, and be ready for company in ten minutes. It's easy to wash those sleepers. A cruising or walking toddler can be counted on to keep tabletops clean and the dog dish empty. As children get older, there's simple midsummer dustiness, followed by the true grit of building a city (with lake) under the swing set.

This is a *long* battle! Fortunately, a parent's standard of cleanliness modifies as the child ages. You simply cannot spend sixteen years with a damp washcloth in your hand. There's a difference between the lifesaving bathing of a baby and "How could you *possibly* throw mud at each other for twenty minutes?" (The answer to the latter is simple: Both mothers saw the battle begin and then ducked away from their windows in hopes the other would intervene. Those who intervene have to clean all participants.)

I don't believe I ever had a kid get sick from being dirty. *I've* nearly gotten sick from it, but it doesn't seem to harm them. We're talking normal, everyday dirt here—you do have to maintain some standards.

Some of the happiest smiles on my children have shone through the dirtiest faces. One boy spent his two years of nursery school on the dirt pile, digging with a child-sized backhoe. Every day as I shook him out, he told me over and over how much he loved school. Too bad they didn't have a dirt pile in high school.

The worst years for dirt are twelve to fifteen years for boys and nine to twelve years for girls. At this stage they don't get covered with as much mud, but they never really get clean, either. They're too old to be scrubbed by Mommy and too young to trust, so you sneak around, trying to peek into their ears while they're otherwise occupied. You feel their toothbrushes when they go to bed to see if they're wet. It takes a kid one evening to learn to run his toothbrush under the tap. In two evenings he learns to run the shower for ten minutes while he sits on the toilet and reads a comic and then ducks his head under the water to get it damp.

Buck up. They are showing great ingenuity in their efforts to stay gamey, and the battle's almost over. One fine evening you're going to hear the shower running for half an hour. The hormones have kicked in! Now peer pressure will take over for you and you can throw away that shabby wet washcloth you've been carrying around for years.

Father, give me the patience I need in this matter of dirt. Keep me cheerful. Let me smile instead of gritting my teeth or speaking out in anger when my child is happily dirty. Remind me there is no shame in the dust of hard work and that right now my child's play is his work.

Pleasant words are as an honeycomb, sweet to the soul, and health to the bones.

Proverbs 16:24

19

No

We believed in discipline when our kids were little, and in later years it paid off, but it takes discrimination. Start off with your basic lifesaving discipline designed to assure the child's safe arrival in kindergarten. Most of this revolves around the word *no*.

You have to realize there are at least three levels of meaning for the word *no*. Level one is the long, drawn out, low-pitched *no* that warns "I see you looking at that vase, but don't touch it." Quite often that's followed by level two, a shorter, sharper, louder *no* that translates "Hands off that vase, kid!" Level three, which soon follows, is a high-pitched, ear-splitting "No. No, no. *NO!*" This means "Don't throw that vase at Grandma or I won't be responsible for what happens to you."

A one-year-old is perfectly capable of understanding all three levels, plus a few more specialized ones developed by his individual family. For the first couple of years the word *no* suffices nicely for discipline.

The trick is to use it as seldom as possible so it retains its effectiveness. In a fairly well baby-proofed house, it's not necessary to spend the day forbidding a baby his destructive little pleasures. Save your *nos* for the important things like avoiding hot ovens and not pulling out Aunt Ellen's pierced earrings.

It's important to stick by your *nos* when you do say them. At any level of urgency a *no* is a *no* and must be obeyed. A clearly understood shake of the head is as valid as a level-three scream, and the child must understand that you will always enforce your *nos*. Even if he throws a tantrum in the supermarket (and he will), he is still not going to be allowed to squish every grape on the counter.

Luckily parents are bigger and stronger than babies. An ignored *no* requires physical restraint or a lightly slapped hand. It doesn't require long lectures, adult temper tantrums, or harshness—just firmness.

Babies aren't stupid. Soon you won't have to say no when he gets near the oven or Aunt Ellen's tantalizing earrings. Disapproving looks or head shakes will begin to work, leaving the word *no* for the important matters of life and death. You have one vital goal here: You have to get a child trained to obey your *nos* before he begins to walk well, because soon he'll be faster than you. Then it's only a matter of time before he makes a break for the road. You'll see him two seconds before he plunges off the curb, yell a level-three *NO!* and see him stop on a dime without thinking. It's a wonderful word when it works.

I don't like being told no any more than my baby, Lord, but help me to teach him patiently and lovingly that a no *is a* no, *now and forevermore. Give me discrimination and a light but firm hand in this task, for the sake of his safety.*

Now no chastening for the present seemeth to be joyous, but grievous: nevertheless afterward it yieldeth the peaceable fruit of righteousness unto them which are exercised thereby.

Hebrews 12:11

20

Potty

Somewhere between the ages of one and two a baby will begin to show an interest in being toilet trained. It may be as subtle as a pained expression when you've been too busy to change him right away, or it could be more graphic.

The kid is ready. Maybe he's as sick of diapers as you. Maybe he has an older brother he wants to imitate. Maybe he wants a pair of pants with a real zipper. Who cares why? Take the offered opportunity and run with it, because it's a passing chance, at best.

This is another long process, no matter how easy it seems at first. True, there are no technical skills required of either of you. There's no pressure involved, as long as you discount half of what the other mothers you know are claiming (always a good idea). It's still a long process.

Invest in a potty chair. Get the little fellow's attention and ask if he really wants to do this. If he says yes, show him you're happy. If he says no, convince him he really *means* yes. Explain all the benefits to him, put him on the potty (don't forget the deflector for little boys—it's *vital*), find a beloved book, and read your little heart out.

Sometimes you get lucky. Sometimes you get this perverse thought that he's training you and, early on, he is. You're just there at the right time. This stage is a snap, outside of the little impression he gets on his fanny and the discomfort you have from sitting on the edge of the bathtub for too long. *Hint:* When you're uncomfortable, so is he. Put the diaper back on and try later.

Being a smart little fellow, he soon catches on. You can see it in his eyes; he *knows* what's expected of him. Now comes the stalemate. He won't tell you when. Why should he? You're nicely trained to anticipate him, aren't you? You know he eventually will do it himself, as not many boys go to college in their diapers, no matter how probable that looks now. But he doesn't want to give in, and he has longer to live than you.

At this point make a big show of giving up and letting him win. Be reasonable and kind, put the diaper back on, and don't mention the potty again until he does. Put it away somewhere. It throws him off balance and saves your sanity.

Sooner or later, he will mention it. I found one of ours sitting quietly on his potty, fully dressed, reading a book in his room. Go back to explaining how he has to tell you when. One day soon he will. Believe it or not, the battle is won at this point. No, he's not trained yet. Yes, he'll turn stubborn at least three times a day. But he knows now, and he gave in once, so he has no more pride to protect. Somewhere around three, he'll really be trained, except maybe at night.

Are little girls easier to train than boys? Yes and no. They seem to be interested earlier and make an effort to please you, so the stalemate may be of shorter duration. But they use a different technique to break you, and it's harder to resist them—at least it was for me. You also have to lug around a lot less equipment for little boys, bushes being their favorite training site! Just don't let it get to you or come between you and your child. It's not that important.

Lord, I don't like it when my child and I have a clash of wills. We can both be so stubborn and foolish! When I find myself falling into the trap of sheer stubbornness, remind me that he's only a baby and nothing is important enough to justify my treating him harshly or unfeelingly. Give me the insight I need to guide him surely, calmly, and always with love.

The Lord is gracious, and full of compassion; slow to anger, and of great mercy.

Psalms 145:8

21 Axioms: Two to Three Years

A two-year-old wakes up from his nap exactly five minutes after you begin yours.

The day your long-awaited family vacation begins at least one child will have a fever.

The first song your child sings will be from a TV commercial.

The first joke your child tells will involve a bodily function.

Any toy your child wants will be at the bottom of the toy box.

No child willingly drinks water until after he is put to bed for the night.

22

You have a two-year-old? You have my sympathy. At the same time, I envy you. I'm too old to deal with a two-year-old full-time now, but I remember them with fondness, now that they're grown.

I love the bodies of two-year-olds. Their legs have almost caught up with their torsos, so they're not so top-heavy and not as likely to trip over the pattern in the kitchen floor. They're compact and perfectly formed for hugging, but so full of energy. Even when they're asleep you can see the energy rippling through their muscles.

At two you can even take them to a real restaurant, if you're brave enough. I think our daughter was two when we took her to a quiet restaurant at the shore for an early dinner. Being temporarily an only child, she was used to the company of adults and her manners were respectable for her age. Everyone there made a big fuss over her, which she accepted as her due. We gave the waitress our order, and in the split second of silence before the waitress left, Laura brushed a leftover crumb off her placemat and exclaimed in her clearest diction, "Dirty, dirty, Mommy!"

62   From Training Pants to Training Wheels

By the time the two boys came along, we'd been reduced to fast-food restaurants for a dinner out. Once they outnumber you, you learn to take precautions.

Two-year-olds bleed a lot. Anyone who moves that fast with so little control has lots of collisions with stationary objects—perfectly visible, harmless stationary objects. The doorknobs in our house kept attacking one of our boys. Another son kept forgetting about the half wall between the dining room and the living room and met it the hard way more than once. Stairs pathologically hate two-year-olds and trip them up anytime you're not looking.

Two-year-olds have a rapidly growing vocabulary, most of it picked up from other kids, adults, and TV. Their pronunciation isn't perfect, but you'll recognize the words that need erasing (usually in public).

By now they know exactly what the word *no* means and are in the process of seeing how far they can stretch your patience before they're in physical danger. They appropriate the word for their own use far too often for their own good.

At the end of this year some children graduate to a real bed that's outfitted with a plastic mattress cover and a removable metal safety bar. The exact timing of this event varies. Children who sleep peacefully through the night or have a baby brother or sister on the way move earlier than only children who are night stalkers. Whenever it happens, don't fool yourself: No plastic is going to save that mattress, and every child falls out of bed once a night for the first six months. They also manage to crawl to the bottom of the bed and entangle themselves in the covers with regularity. The resulting muffled howls scare the heck out of you at 2:00 A.M.

Two-year-old girls love to be ladies, dressing up, sitting quietly, and trying to copy the letters that form their names. They want to draw and color. They sing TV commercials off-key in the sweetest of voices. They can be utterly charming for long periods, as long as there's only one of them in the room. Put two of them together and it's mud wrestling time!

Two-year-old boys couldn't care less about being gentlemen and drawing or coloring. They drive trucks all day on the floor. If there are two or more of them in the room, they drive their trucks into each other and get into fights like good truck drivers.

Rituals are vitally important to children at this age. If you always feed your child a boiled egg for breakfast, don't try to introduce scrambled eggs this year or you'll wreck his life. If Daddy always does the bedtime bathing, you'd better hope he doesn't have to leave town until the child is three. The two-year-old wants everything to stay the same, day after day—while he changes his mind every five minutes!

Luckily, most two-year-olds still nap once a day. The most blissful hour of the day, it's the only time you can possibly take a bath, iron a shirt, call a friend, or, better yet, take a nap yourself. You'll need it; it's a long year.

Protector of all the little animals, we need You around here this year! I run out of Band-Aids once a week. I kiss skinned elbows and knees daily, wipe away tears of frustration and anger hourly, endure temper tantrums and cries in the night. Our lives are emotional roller coasters this year, Lord. Keep me rooted in Your love and security, so I may do the same for my family.

When I said, My foot slippeth; thy mercy, O Lord, held me up. In the multitude of my thoughts within me thy comforts delight my soul.

Psalms 94:18, 19

23

New Baby

We have pictures of our two oldest children that speak louder than a Methodist choir sings. In the first, our oldest is looking down at our second baby with curiosity and distaste. She's scratching her head absentmindedly; she's not impressed. She had wanted a sister, and we'd brought home a boy by mistake. Was he returnable?

In the second photo the baby in the first picture is looking at our third child. There's no doubt about his thoughts: "Couldn't you do any better than *that?*" He'd gotten the brother he'd wanted, only to find out he wasn't good for much.

Things have gotten better, but I still see those looks on their faces now and then. As I was an only child, I can't share that pain with them, but I know it's real pain. We'd hurt them deeply by bringing these noisy, demanding, time-consuming creatures into their lives. We'd changed their lives, upset their routines, and relegated them to the status of "Just a minute." On top of it all we expected them to love and protect these interlopers! I would feel the same if my husband brought home a skinny twenty-five-year-old and told me she was here to stay!

Some children lie better than others. They may even convince their parents they love their new brother and aren't in the least upset by his presence. I preferred it when mine looked me in the eye and said, "You don't love me anymore." At least I had the chance to tell them they were wrong, to reassure them I still loved them, even if they thought I was lying.

It gets better as the baby develops a little personality and mobility. Our second child was smart enough to smile at his sister first. She could climb up, peer over the edge of his crib, and take him from indignant crying to hysterical laughter before I even got to his room. He was a good audience. He was also a good student for a three-year-old girl who knew all about trucks, pets, crayons, and getting around parents. Once she found he was a docile, worshipful younger brother, she pronounced him keepable.

The third wasn't all that docile, and not at all worshipful, but that was okay with the second. Once he learned how to throw a toy with authority, he was accepted into the male fraternity and protected until he could protect himself.

I want them to grow up to be friends. I want them to call one another when something wonderful or terrible happens in their lives. I want their children to know and fight with one another, like real cousins should. I want them to stay a family long after I'm gone. Even though they're still calling one another names, I have high hopes for them.

Lord, help these children of mine have that deep-down love for one another that comes from being family. As different as they are, they are in a sense one, and that oneness is a source of strength and courage if they know how to claim it. Show them how, Lord.

Be kindly affectioned one to another with brotherly love; in honour preferring one another.

Romans 12:10

24

Guilt

I'm so glad the days of Super Mom are over. The end didn't come in time to save me, but maybe my daughter will be able to live without the burden of guilt my generation carried on its back for twenty years.

Being a full-time mother went out of style sometime between the births of my second and third children. I was raised and trained to be a wife and mother, back there in the fifties. It was considered an honorable profession then. I had just settled into domesticity and taken out a subscription to *Ladies' Home Journal* when the rules changed. Everyone started telling me I now had to get a *real* job and farm out my children for eight hours a day. The second part of the edict sounded tempting, but I wasn't ready for the first.

First, who would want to hire me? What corporation needed a first-class diaper changer? Coping with a toddler requires a lot of tact and energy, but not the kind needed in the business world. Hair pulling I could handle; back-stabbing was an alien skill.

Second, I enjoyed what I was doing and they were all eating and growing, anyway. I truly liked being a mother and resented the implication that I was wasting my life. I begged the whole question by promptly having a third child. *That* would show them!

But the articles kept appearing, telling women of my generation we could do it all. We could become vice-presidents and raise wonderful children at the same time. It was nice of them to be so confident in us, but which one of them was going to come in and scrub the oatmeal off the wall while I worked at becoming a vice-president?

According to them, my husband would help. He would find it fulfilling to take the baby to the pediatrician and run a few loads of laundry on the side. Bull! Don't get me wrong; he did help a lot. But he wasn't brought up to be a househusband any more than I was to be a vice-president. There were limits to his capabilities and time, since he was going to have to support us while I worked my way out of the mailroom.

So I stayed home and lived with my guilt until my youngest was going to school full-time. Then I caved in to the Super Mom mentality and got a job. Maybe I could have it all; a lot of women apparently did.

This is where we get into major guilt. There were many

days I had to send a barely healthy child off to school and wait for the nurse to call. If he were really sick, Bill and I would fight over who got to go to work. My kids couldn't bring friends home after school. They depended on the kindness of other mothers to get to ball games and after-school lessons. They called me at the office to say there were no snacks and it looked like it was going to thunder and the dog was scared of thunder and when would I be home?

Eventually I came to my senses. I didn't want to be anyone's vice-president, so why was I killing myself and missing out on all the fun at home? I went back to the job I really loved—being a mother. And guilt came home with me. But I don't care anymore. Guilt's welcome in my house now, as long as his feet aren't muddy.

I hope it's easier for my daughter.

Sometimes we have to tell society to get lost and live our lives the way we want to, Lord. But it's never easy bucking a trend. Help me when these decisions have to be made. Let me listen to Your voice before I listen to someone else.

Hearken now unto my voice, I will give thee counsel, and God shall be with thee. . . .

Exodus 18:19

25

"Me Do It!"

All children develop differently, but most learn that sentence very well between the ages of two and three years. It's good because he's developing independence and learning new skills; on the other hand, he (and you) need to wake up an hour earlier to allow him time to dress himself.

Letting a child do anything by himself at this age is a test of patience, yours and his. He wants to dress himself but it takes him five minutes to get his pants on the wrong way. Half the time his shoes go on the wrong foot, and there's nothing more furious than a two-year-old with his head stuck in the neck hole of a sweatshirt.

If you make the mistake of asking "Do you want me to help?" you'll be answered with tears of outrage. And yet you can't leave him to do it alone, because he *can't*. Mothers going through this phase of life successfully should be awarded diplomatic posts in the Third World, for they can handle anything.

Children this age end up having two baths daily: One they give themselves and one Mother sneaks in. "Here's a little spot you can't reach. Let me do it for you." It's amazing how fast a mother can scrub a whole tiny body when given an opportunity.

Sneakiness is important to your well-being. No two-

From Training Pants to Training Wheels

year-old can cut up hamburger meat, although they all will insist on doing it, if given the chance. So you cut it up at the stove with your back turned and present it as a fait accompli. He won't notice. He'll be too busy telling his father he can put the catsup on by himself. When it's time for him to brush his teeth, you will keep him busy wetting the brush while you apply the toothpaste. You get the idea.

Dawdling is a time-honored tradition for two-year-olds. You may have to get out of the house at a given time, but he doesn't. He can't tell time, so it has no meaning to him. Every morning, all over the country, there are half-naked two-year-olds playing with cars on their bedroom floors two minutes before their parents have to leave the house. Two minutes is the absolute limit. Cut it any closer and he'll arrive at the sitter's in bare feet or unmatched socks. As it is, he'll still arrive crying and furious at you for finishing his dressing in record time, but at least he'll be decent.

You deal with it with gritted teeth. You plan ahead, leave extra time for anything involving his helping himself, and learn to distract him while you finish whatever he started. If you plan things in advance, you'll have the needed time for him to do it himself. If you don't, you'll take the consequences. If ever there was a time for patience and a sense of humor, this is it.

Lord, day after day I tell myself I will have patience; I will be a teacher, not a nagger. But day after day I nag, because my patience and my time are so limited. I know it takes time for him to learn to do things. How nice it would be if he were pleasant about it, though. Patience—grant me great gobs of patience, Lord.

I know thy works, and thy labour, and thy patience. . . .

Revelation 2:2

26

The Mother's Curse

Sometime during your child's terrible twos you're going
to remember The Mother's Curse. You'll flash back to your
own teenage years and hear your mother's fateful words:
"I hope you have as much trouble with your children as
you gave me!"

Christians don't believe in earthly curses, but this one is
different. It works! Not because it's a curse but because the
laws of heredity and averages come to bear on every
generation.

Your sweet, loving mother, trying to drink her coffee
while balancing a wriggling, screaming grandchild on her
lap, will suddenly get an inappropriate, satisfied look on
her face—*and you'll know.* Your patient father will toss
your son over his shoulder and carry him back to bed
(again), flashing you a look of quiet triumph—*and you'll
know.*

You have to use restraint here. You can't go around
accusing your parents of cursing you, even if you're all

From Training Pants to Training Wheels

aware of what's going on. Right now they're probably the only people willing to baby-sit for you, for one thing. They're also having a lot of fun watching you squirm, and if you're honest, you'll admit they deserve their fun.

It will be a few years before you're tempted to use the curse yourself. When it's time you will have to make your own decision about saying the words or swallowing them. I have a feeling it's more satisfying to say them, but you're the one who has to live with the results.

Father, I know I wasn't too easy on my parents, but this two-year-old is certainly teaching me to appreciate what I must have put them through. My own parenthood is bringing me so much closer to my parents, helping us become friends as well as family. Thank You for that.

Children's children are the crown of old men; and the glory of children are their fathers.

Proverbs 17:6

27

Toys

Let's get down to the good stuff, the things that keep your children occupied so you can clean the bathtub before it grows green slime.

During the first year you have time for the slime because the baby sleeps most of the year. The toys required at this age are simple: a rattle, a mobile, and a stuffed animal to drool on. Babies really don't have the time or talent to play. Of course, you're too tired to do much cleaning during this year, but the time is there, if you can claim it.

The two years that follow go by in a blur. You spend them close on the heels of a crawling, cruising, toddling baby who can't be trusted the minute you turn your back. Now is the time to find some absorbing toys! I worked on the principle of the simpler, the better, such as solid, one-piece toys with nothing that can be pulled or chewed off; toys that don't hurt too much when they hit you in the head; toys that can be spit up on and washed six times a day.

If I had work to do in the kitchen, the toys were pots and pans and wooden spoons and those wonderful plastic food containers. In the bathroom there were brushes, rolls of toilet paper, and soft haircurlers. In our bedroom there were pillows to climb over and plastic thirty-five-millimeter film containers. These were the kinds of toys

From Training Pants to Training Wheels

my kids loved. They would ignore the most expensive dump truck in the world if they could have a tasty wooden spoon.

At this age the ultimate toy is a pet. A cat or dog provides hours of amusement for a toddler. He will watch the animal, stalk the animal, and torment the animal for hours on end. Our dogs always put up with the children. They would look at us with those martyr eyes but would never bite or snap. We spent a lot of time rescuing our dogs. On the other hand, there are cats. Babies don't know the difference between the two at first, but they learn fast. Our cats took no nonsense from children: Look, but don't touch, was their rule.

Preschool years bring "educational" toys. All preschoolers are geniuses. If you think about all they're learning and how fast they learn it, that's a true statement. You have to forgive the parent of a preschooler for bragging, even if you know her little Tommy is a bit on the slow side when compared to your Eleanor.

The only people in the world who buy so-called educational toys for their children are the parents of preschoolers. Preschoolers have bookcases full of books they can't read. They own boxes of crayons that are used mostly for a three-o'clock snack when no one is looking. They possess four different colors of Play-Doh and make absolutely nothing but a mess with it. They use their beautiful blocks as weapons or to clog up every toilet in the house. The best toy I ever found for a preschooler was another preschooler. The possibilities are endless, and they never wear out or seriously break.

Parents of older preschoolers insist their children play outside "in the good, healthy air." Good air has nothing to do with it. You've just cleaned the floor for the fourth time in one day and will throttle the next child who throws a toy on it, so you send them outside to destroy the neighborhood. Let them spread clay on little Mike's new bedspread for a change—if Mike's mother lets them in the house!

Toys are necessary and wonderful, as long as you don't build your child's life around them or become enslaved to them. Any child would rather spend a half hour in his mother's lap than play with a fifty-dollar toy.

Lord, You know that even a child can be a materialist, shouting "I want, I want." As a mother, I want my child to have the things that bring him joy, so I give in too often, even if it is out of love. Help me to discriminate in my giving. Help me to remember to give more of myself and less of things and to teach my child the true value of the immaterial and everlasting as he grows.

Or what man is there of you, whom if his son ask bread, will he give him a stone? Or if he asks a fish, will he give him a serpent? If ye then, being evil, know how to give good gifts unto your children, how much more shall your Father which is in heaven give good things to them that ask him?

Matthew 7:9–11

From Training Pants to Training Wheels

28 Playgrounds

Back in the days when Bill Cosby was being funny on records instead of TV, he told a story about playgrounds that raised the serious question, "Why are my parents trying to kill me?"

It's a valid question. Why do we drag our children away from their blocks, books, and blankets and take them to crowded, noisy, dirty places known as playgrounds? Kids don't *like* playgrounds, at least not when their parents are sitting on a bench watching them play.

It's okay when they're babies, all immobilized in blankets, squinting up through the leaves at the sun. You take them for the fresh air and the chance to look modest when the retirees playing checkers coo and gurgle over your pride and joy. That's good for everyone involved.

As the baby turns into a toddler, your motivation changes. *You* need to get out in the fresh air, someplace where your child can't do permanent damage to anything. But what does the toddler get out of it?

In our playground he got attacked by Canada geese and collected goose poop on his sneakers. He didn't think either was much fun. I'd put him into one of those shipping crates on chains they call a toddler swing, give him a few pushes, and stand back in case he lost his lunch. Then I'd place him on top of the slide so his bare legs would stick to the metal and burn. After a few minutes of playing with used Popsicle sticks in the sandbox, he'd reach his limits of endurance and I would feel totally depraved and guilty.

Kids are tough, though. If you keep it up, they can adjust to anything. In a year he was chasing the geese with a look of vengeance, gulping down the bread I gave him for the geese, and cackling with glee.

He'll get back at you, too. Instead of sticking to the slide and crying, he now comes down headfirst to hear you scream. He throws sandbox sand into the hair of any little girl in range. He refuses to learn how to pump the swing, so you have to stand there and listen to him demand, "Higher, Mommy!" while you get nauseated from watching him.

Another year—you're a real glutton for punishment, aren't you? He's on his own now, climbing like a monkey to the top of the Jungle Gym. If you're lucky, you won't see who started the spitting contest up there. If you did see, you'd be a fool to admit it. You carry Band-Aids in your purse, along with the telephone number of the paramedics. You dress him in a bright red T-shirt, so you can see if he's at the top or bottom of the pileup in the fight. You pray for rain and snow. You start looking for a good nursery school, because playgrounds really aren't safe places for parents anymore.

How easy it is to measure his growth by his reach on the Jungle Gym, Lord. From a tentative first handhold to a heart-stopping

From Training Pants to Training Wheels

*leap takes such a short time. Remind me to enjoy these years while
I can.*

> . . . Let the young men now arise, and play before us.
>
> 2 Samuel 2:14

29 Nightmares

It's hard to be calm when you're woken at 2:00 A.M. by
screams of terror coming from your child's room. My
husband, who wakes up if a pin drops, would hear them
first. But he operated on the theory that there was nothing
to worry about until I was worried, and I sleep like a log.
By the time I heard them, the whole neighborhood did,
too, and the concerned child was approaching hysteria.

I'd stumble into the room, my heart pounding, switch
on the light, and try to comfort the screamer with plati-
tudes: "Shh. It's only a dream. It's not real. Mommy's
here. Shh."

Sometimes it worked. It depended on the child. Our
oldest had nightmares often, but like her father, she woke
up easily and could be comforted. All I needed to do for
her was check under the bed, in the closet, and behind the
stuffed animals. A drink of water later, she'd be soundly
asleep.

If our second child had nightmares, he kept them to

himself. I don't recall him waking us up once. Maybe he enjoyed them, like he enjoys horror movies today. Maybe he just slept through them and never noticed. He was always a stoic who kept quiet when he should have yelled.

Then there was Steven, blessed with a vivid imagination and the ability to sleep through *anything*. In the grips of a nightmare, he would be so out of it that my husband learned to wake me early in the process.

"Steve's having a nightmare," he'd whisper, poking me into consciousness.

"Screaming?"

"Not yet. He's just started thrashing and talking."

We'd both go in, hoping to wake him before the dream progressed too far. If we were extremely lucky, we'd be able to shake him awake before his incoherent mutterings turned into screams.

Most of the time we couldn't wake him in time and would be faced with stark terror. He'd bolt upright in bed, sweat pouring off him, his eyes wide open and unseeing.

We could talk to him, walk him, hug him, nothing registered. He'd shake us off and go on yelling. He scared the heck out of us!

In time we'd begin to get replies to our questions. Not that they made any sense, but it was a step in the right direction. Then he'd stop screaming and accept a drink of water. Next would come coherent replies and suddenly he would see us there.

His nightmares must have been doozies! We'll never know, though. Once he was finally awake, he could never remember anything about his dream and he didn't wake up afraid or wanting comfort. One minute he was blotto,

From Training Pants to Training Wheels

the next he was smiling and secure, asking if it were morning yet. I could have killed him!

I still remember the nightmares of my youth, Lord. What powerful events they must be! And how my child scares me now when he wakes with one. Please teach me how to handle these fears of his, how to lessen their impact and bring Your peace to my trembling child, because nothing hurts me as much as seeing my child hurt.

Then thou scarest me with dreams, and terrifiest me through visions.

Job 7:14

30 Axioms: Three to Four Years

Any three-year-old who can pour his own milk will knock over the glass as soon as it's filled.

Never walk in on a little boy in the bathroom. He may turn around at the wrong time.

A three-year-old believes in Santa Claus, ghosts, the Easter Bunny, monsters, God, and goblins. Only the bad ones hide under his bed.

All dogs bite—except yours.

Band-Aids heal all invisible wounds.

All knock-down, drag-out fights can be mediated with chocolate chip cookies.

31

Three

Everything goes fast when you have a three-year-old. His little legs really work by three—all day long! He can go up and down stairs by himself and will, unless you've invested in one of those gates that pinch your fingers every time you try to put it up (any three-year-old can open such gates with alacrity). If you stop him from climbing the stairs, he will climb something else just as dangerous and much more breakable.

Since his legs are so functional, you'll probably buy your three-year-old a shiny red tricycle or a Big Wheel. This is an understandable mistake you will soon regret, once you get over admiring your child's new freedom. Face it: At three a child is too young to treat freedom with respect. A three-year-old on a tricycle believes the road was put there just for him and has no qualms about fighting an eighteen-wheeler for the right of way. Spring and summer make up only a small part of the year; the snow and rain will come soon enough, and you will be stuck with a child deprived of his wheels.

Three-year-olds don't handle deprivation well. Unless

you want to stand out in a blizzard and watch him chug around the driveway, you will give in and carry the vehicle into the house. This makes for one of the noisiest, busiest winters of your life. You'll spend a good part of it patching the paint job you just finished in the downstairs hall.

Three-year-olds have neighborhood friends who also have trikes they want to ride inside your house. You can fight this if you want and insist they all share your child's vehicle, but a three-year-old's friends aren't all that nice and you will spend the winter breaking up fistfights unless you give in and accept the fleet. Once your teeth get numb from the noise, it's sort of fun watching them play bumper cars in your kitchen.

A three-year-old can obey simple commands along the lines of "Go find Daddy and tell him I need him." Unfortunately, he also can obey "Go find Mommy and tell her I'm busy." This comes in handy if you have another baby in the house and need to say, "Go get a clean diaper and bring it to me." A three-year-old loves to run errands for you as much as a teenage boy loves to use a new driver's license. Sometimes he'll forget the second half of the request and you'll find him using the clean diaper to scrub the trike, but it's a start.

Although they seem fearless when you wish they would be careful, three-year-olds develop irrational fears of their own (irrational only to adults). Our daughter was terrified of big friendly dogs, who all seemed to love her. When you're three, any dog is a big dog. We had a son who was afraid of ghosts. As far as I knew, there weren't any ghosts in our house, but he looked for them for a whole year. The third needed a light on in the hall or he wouldn't go to sleep. I could live with that, but his older brother couldn't stand having a light on in the hall while *he* went to sleep, and hall lights don't discriminate.

A three-year-old likes to function on his own whenever possible. He wants to undress himself. Since most of them can't manage to take their tops off alone but do very well with their pants, they tend to appear at your dinner parties in a most embarrassing condition. Our neighbors' three-year-old would let himself out of the house early in the morning and come to visit us half-naked (in the winter). We looked forward to his visits, but his parents put a lock way up high on the door and by the time he had mastered that, he was old enough to remember his pants when he visited.

They are so smart, so fast, so noisy at three. Best of all, when they get tired and slow down, they're perfectly willing to snuggle up and let you read them a story, steal a kiss or two, and stock up on hugs. You can never stock up on too many hugs when you're a parent—you run out by the time they hit their teens—so enjoy them now.

Lord of the shadows, Ruler of the dark place under the bed, help me calm my child's fears this year. Give me the wisdom to teach him to trust You for protection from the monsters his active mind creates, day and night, asleep or awake. At the same time, Lord, build into him a little common sense about the real, human dangers of this world, without squelching his natural love of life and people. Take my child in Your arms and bless him this year.

And he took them up in his arms, put his hands upon them, and blessed them.

Mark 10:16

From Training Pants to Training Wheels

32

Last Christmas I gave each of our children, who are now into or past their teens, their own photo albums prestocked with their own baby pictures. I was thus able to thin out some of my dusty photo albums while at the same time giving the children something that was rightfully theirs—their childhood memories.

Photography is a subject of conflict in our family, the one activity guaranteed to drive Bill and me into sullenness and loud words (he gets sullen, I get loud). To me, an event doesn't happen unless it produces pictures (i.e., prints) I can hold, study, send to relatives, and subsequently lose. Bill, on the other hand, takes slides I can never see unless I make him set up the projector, which is another sporting event. He knows how to take pictures with a thirty-five-millimeter camera that all but talks. All I can do is push a button and cut off people's heads. But I at least have film in *my* camera; he uses up his photographing birds. As you can see, it's a sore subject all around.

But we're fairly normal parents, and we have tons of pictures of Laura in the form of slides, prints, and movies. We have pictures of everything she did from birth to age nine.

Jim has lots of pictures from his birth to age three, but no movies. The movie camera died and never was replaced.

Steve has one miserable page with most of the pictures showing an older brother and sister hogging the camera.

This is so typical that everyone takes it for granted and jokes about it, but it wasn't funny last Christmas. The farther down the ladder, the fewer pictures of the child. It's got to make him wonder.

It's all perfectly nondiscriminatory and logical: The more kids you have, the less time you have for taking pictures. And events seem to photograph the same for each child. You see one kid reading on the potty, you've seen them all.

Except that you haven't. Each of them reads on the potty in his own individual style, and Laura was the only one so captured. I missed two wonderful pictures because I didn't know that in time. I missed Halloween costumes, Little League games, birthday parties, and summer vacations. They're gone forever, with no pictures to bring them back, just because it was an effort to take pictures and we thought we had seen it all before.

So I'm putting this right up with the three-year-old stories, figuring you're about ready to put your camera on the closet shelf. Don't do it; keep it on the kitchen counter, and keep on faithfully taking pictures of everything for the next twenty years. You won't get any second chances at this, so don't blow it now!

Dear Lord, it's hard to do things for the future when the present is so busy, but make me try. I remember to save for my child's education. Help me to save memories for myself, memories I'll need when they grow up and move away the day after tomorrow.

From Training Pants to Training Wheels

And that these days should be remembered and kept throughout every generation, every family, every province, and every city. . . .

Esther 9:28

33

Television

I'm not a television snob. Television didn't pollute my children's minds; other kids did that for them. As far as I can see, television was good for my children.

I did have my standards and always kept an ear to what was coming from the TV, but life was simpler when my kids were three. There was no cable then and no remote control. My three-year-olds had to ask me to change channels for them, the channel knob being difficult for their little hands to move. For the most part, their viewing was limited to cartoons, "Sesame Street," and "The Electric Company," most of which I enjoyed as much as they. There was nothing like a visit with Mr. Rogers to even out my day and prepare me for the dinner hour.

Television taught my children to count to ten: "One, two, three, **four**, five" ("Sesame Street"). It taught them to recognize certain words by sight: "I'm the plumber, and

I've come to fix the sink" ("The Electric Company"). My twenty-two-year-old daughter can still sing the opening song to "Mister Rogers' Neighborhood," and it still makes her feel loved.

I think the reason I feel so good about children and TV is that we had such good times watching it together. My daughter and I watched "Lassie" at 7:00 P.M. every Sunday night, sitting close to each other on the couch. We sat close because at the darkest moment, when there was no way Lassie could find her way back to Timmy, we'd both start to sniffle. And although we knew it would only make things worse, we would look at each other's overflowing eyes and give in to a good sob or two. Then we would comfort each other and say it would be okay. Every Sunday this three-year-old and I would subject ourselves to this. It felt good to us both.

I can't say we feel the same closeness now when watching MTV together. I don't understand the songs, and she won't explain them to me. But all in all, TV did some good things for our family.

Father, help me use whatever comes our way as a positive influence in our family's life, for there are lessons to be passed on about all of life. Tragedy or comedy, real life or TV, let me use them all wisely, for whatever good they can give us.

. . . shewing to the generation to come the praises of the Lord, and his strength, and his wonderful works that he hath done.

Psalms 78:4

From Training Pants to Training Wheels

34

If there is one thing a child always needs, it's a good bath. From the day you bring him home until he discovers the opposite sex, a child is gamey, dusty, greasy, and capable of growing potatoes in his ears. I used to wonder if God was trying to tell me this was his natural condition; maybe I shouldn't be fooling with Mother Nature? Then I realized it was *my* bed he was climbing into in the middle of the night, and Mother Nature was going to have to adjust, not me.

Generally, the tinier the child, the easier he is to clean. This is true for several reasons: It takes less swipes with a washcloth to cover the skin area of a seven-pounder than of a twenty-five-pounder (the difference between basting a Sunday chicken and a Thanksgiving turkey); the bigger he gets, the faster he moves; the bigger he gets, the less help he'll accept from you; the bigger he gets, the more varieties of dirt he will find in one day.

Nothing in the world is as frightening as bathing a new baby. It takes total organization and nerves of steel. If you're smart, you will draft your husband to help out. Even then four hands are barely sufficient. One hand holds his wobbly head, the second, his wriggling body, the third soaps him up, and the fourth rinses. I needed a fifth hand to shoo away the cat, who always wondered what kind of animal I was trying to drown in the kitchen sink. Yes, the kitchen sink, with its big basin, handy counter area, and sprayer, is the perfect place to wash basin-sized babies.

Once you and the baby both learn to relax, bathtime becomes fun. You discover he's ticklish under the arms; he discovers he can splash you with impunity. You both end up soaked and laughing.

Bathing toddlers is equally rewarding. This is the age of the bathtub flotilla of plastic toys that makes it hard to find, let alone scrub, your child's feet. You have to make an executive decision at this point: Wash first and play later, or vice versa? Or you can cop out, as I did, and wash in the middle, which gives them soaking time before and rinsing time after.

In no time at all it seemed I had a crowd in the tub— three of them of various ages and sexes—having a wonderful time playing while I washed whatever body part was above water and reachable at the time. It was bedlam but they loved it, and it was certainly more sensible than three separate baths. The only hard part was drying three at once. One always escaped and ran for the back door stark naked, to test my reaction time.

The next step is that of the supervised self-bather, who calls you in before pulling the plug (if you're lucky). While you cry in amazement, "Oh, look how clean you got yourself today!" you grab a washcloth and rapidly scrub the dirtiest parts of his anatomy without letting him know what you're doing. (How? Keep him talking and work fast!)

Soon he won't let you in at all. You will have to wait downstairs until he appears in his pajamas for inspection.

His pajamas will be clinging to his body because he never thinks to use a towel. The only part of him you can still wash at this point are his ears, and that's a fight.

After this stage he's on his own, which means he'll never be truly clean until he becomes a teenager and starts taking thirty-minute showers.

There's no doubt that bathtime is a strenuous activity. Try to convince your husband it's "quality time" *he* should be having with the children while you read the evening paper!

Sometimes, Lord, I'd rather give up and let him go to bed dirty. I'm tired at bathtime, the floor tiles hurt my knees, and my back is getting too old to be mistreated like this. But when he's cleaned up and smells of baby shampoo, he certainly is nice to hug!

. . . and he that hath clean hands shall be stronger and stronger.

Job 17:9

35

I don't know about you, but I grew up on the Brothers Grimm and their tales of lurking trolls (never trust a stone bridge) and drooling hobgoblins. I had a lot of nightmares, too! I clearly remember heaving that faithful, worn book into the garbage pail as soon as I was old enough to read. I found something else to read, a book that wasn't out to make me wet the bed.

I wouldn't think of reading a Stephen King book to my kids, so I sure didn't read them fairy tales. They grew up on *Green Eggs and Ham* and *The Cat in the Hat.* Even now, they half expect funny books to rhyme. Dr. Seuss was safe. He was as much fun for me as he was for them, and the illustrations were so full of detail they kept a two-year-old's attention on one page until I got through all the words.

You can tell when you've found a good book. It keeps appearing on your lap well past the point where you and your child have memorized every word. Soon you get so bored with it that you take liberties with the text: You shorten a sentence here, skip another there. It doesn't work. The child will throw you a baleful look and supply patiently (if it's your first offense of the evening) the skipped sentences. Soon you'll be holding one child and one book while he "reads" the book to you.

Buying children's books was fun, especially when they got old enough to come along to the bookstore. We would go crazy. They could have as many as they wanted, on any subject, as long as it was from the children's section and my credit card was still breathing. Sure it was expensive, even then, but it was money well spent. For the next couple of months we would all explore the world together, crowded on the sofa at bedtime. Everyone listened to everyone else's stories, squirmed, punched, elbowed— and learned.

I miss those days. It's fun sitting in the middle of a pile of warm, clean, slightly sleepy children with damp hair. They smell good, their books smell good, and everyone feels good. Those are short years, so use them well.

Creator of all words, help me teach my children to love the adventure of reading, so they will never be lonely when they're alone with a book.

To know wisdom and instruction; to perceive the words of understanding; To receive the instruction of wisdom, justice, and judgment, and equity; To give subtilty to the simple, to the young man knowledge and discretion.

Proverbs 1:2–4

36 Little Legalists

Between the ages of three and four years, many otherwise carefree children turn into legalists. It's something you bring on yourself, so don't try to squirm out of it (not that they'd let you).

You've spent two to three years telling your child, "Only cross on the green," "Look both ways," "Don't talk to strangers," and "No snacks before dinner."

Some days none of it seems to have taken. Then you will scoot through a yellow light and hear a little voice from the backseat mutter, "Uh-oh." If you're on a roll that day, you will just miss the green on the very next light and hear what my husband heard: "Uh-oh, Daddy. You did it *again!*"

He slowed down that day because Laura was convinced a police car was going to take away her daddy at any minute. The boys went through the same phase, but with a vital difference: They encouraged him to go faster, so they could hear the police siren.

It's humiliating to stand on the curb of a busy intersection ready to go and be forcibly held back by a little child who won't budge until you look both ways several times. It's impossible to explain why you can ask a perfect stranger for directions but your child can't.

This is the time of life when you realize what a hypocrite

you are. You go around breaking your own laws every day, but expect your child to obey them. Worse yet, you may try to justify your lawbreaking on the grounds that you're older and wiser and . . . don't bother. It has to be a time of disillusionment for children.

Don't let me disappoint my child during this difficult phase, Lord. There's so much I can do wrong right now. I need to be vigilant and patient so I can be a good example, because I don't want to teach this child to be a hypocrite like me.

Ye are they which justify yourselves before men; but God knoweth your hearts. . . .

Luke 16:15

37

Sex

Don't panic. Children under the age of five years don't want to know too much about sex, anyway. What they do want to know is basic stuff that any parent can handle. Just don't assume you have to give a thorough sex-education lecture the first time the subject comes up. If a kid asks where he came from, assume he wants to know the location of the hospital until proven otherwise.

Kids do notice basic anatomy at a young age. You should explain the topic to both sexes as soon as they start looking worried about it; it will be obvious when it's time, and it's a fairly straightforward, painless conversation.

By the time the harder questions come up, you will probably be expecting another baby, which makes everything pretty neat. Not only does the child get the information he needs, he gets to watch the miracle stretch out Mommy's tummy and feel it kick. He knows in advance why Mommy will be away for a few days and that she will be bringing him back a baby brother or sister. If you're not conveniently pregnant, you may have to visit a neighbor's expecting pet or read your child a good book on the subject.

The discomfort most adults feel with this subject comes because they take sex far too seriously. A set of natural, God-given facts should be explained to a child in the same calm tone of voice used to explain other acts of nature, like thunderstorms and rainbows. You don't want your child to be scared of sex any more than you want him to be afraid of thunder.

Well, I am afraid of thunder, and my kids picked up on that rapidly. As soon as they began to be scared of thunder themselves, I called in my husband, who gave them a reasoned, factual explanation of thunder and helped them see its beauty. If I were scared of sex, I would have asked for his help explaining that, too.

At this age, the main thing is to keep it as simple as possible. You don't have to go into great detail or get tied up trying to teach a preschooler sexual morals. In case you haven't noticed, most preschoolers are neither morally bad nor morally good—they just *are*. They learn more by your example than by your words and will pick up most of your morals from living with you.

Not that there won't be uncomfortable moments. What do you do when a preschooler walks into the bathroom, slings back the shower curtain, and says "Hi!" Say hello and politely ask him to wait for you in the next room. What do you do when your daughter tries to go to the bathroom like your son? Try not to laugh, then explain that eventually she will be able to do things that he won't, such as having babies. What about playing doctor? You just have to explain that they can't play that at your house, just like they can't play catch in your kitchen. Some things are not allowed, and kids understand that.

Luckily, all this doesn't happen at once. You may have months or years between questions. Maybe you will get lucky and the next question will be directed at your husband instead of you. Both parent and child are maturing and learning—it's part of the grand plan.

Father, is there some reason why these questions always come up in the produce aisle of the supermarket or when the pastor has come to call? I'm glad my child is asking me these questions and I'm really doing the best I can with my answers. Help me keep my cool, whatever the situation.

So God created man in his own image, in the image of God created he him; male and female created he them.

And God blessed them, and God said to them, Be fruitful,
and multiply, and replenish the earth, and subdue it. . . .

Genesis 1:27, 28

38

Nursery School

Once your baby is toilet trained, you'll begin to
consider nursery school. He looks so grown-up in his little
jockey shorts and his overalls don't sag in the back
anymore. In short, he has the streamlined look of a real,
competent person. He doesn't run funny, and he seems
ready to mix it up with other three- or four-year-olds.

I usually hung on to my children until they hit three and
a half years. The early threes are a pretty good time.
Somewhere in the middle of that year, however, a child's
Mr. Hyde side reasserts itself (remember two and a half?).
He becomes a chronic whiner. He starts tripping over the
dog when a month ago he could vault over it without
missing a step. If you laugh at his pratfall, you will be
fixed with a beady stare and told, "Don't laugh!" You
won't be allowed to hug your husband either: "Don't do
that!"

At this point you will either decide you can't take it

anymore or it's not fair to expose the nursery school to your child. My later kids went off to nursery school at three and a half. *I* needed it.

With the first one, I hung on until four, not knowing this tyrant phase was normal and not wanting any outsider to judge me by my child when the judgment was sure to be negative.

But at four, you get into the "Why's the sky blue?" phase.

"It's reflecting the color of the ocean."

"How?"

"The clouds bounce the color back. Like a mirror."

"Why?"

"Because they do. Do you want a lollipop?"

"Yes. How's the sky do that?"

"Because that's the way God made it. Do you want to go to the park?"

"No. How'd God make the sky?"

"How'd you like to go to nursery school?"

That's why they invented nursery school.

Nursery school used to be fun. They climbed into the little van and drove out of your life for three wonderful hours. It wasn't too complicated for anyone. Now I understand you have to be sure your child attends the *right* nursery school so he will get into the *right* group in elementary school and go on to the *right* college. Personally, I was happy as long as the kid had fun and didn't bite anyone.

Nursery schools are filled with patient adults who love to help children color, cut and paste, fingerpaint, and make cows out of clay. They couldn't pay me enough to do that for a living, but there are still some saints around.

Going to parent-teacher conferences is fun when kids are this age, because anything your child does is "creative." In elementary school that translates "disruptive" and is not good.

I loved nursery school. My kids learned so much there and came home so tired that they would fall asleep on the floor in the middle of "Sesame Street" and I would have time to start dinner in peace and quiet. Then I would go wake them up and make them play with me until their father came home, because I had actually missed them and wanted their company. Nursery school was good for all of us.

I'll admit it, Lord: I no longer have all the answers for my child and it bothers me. Ever since his birth, I've known so much more than he, but now his questions are too hard and I've had to entrust his mind to strangers. I know this will be good for both of us and actually draw us closer together, so why do I feel so sad as he is driven off? Give me the strength to do what's right for him, Lord, even if it means giving him up a little.

My son, if thou wilt receive my words, and hide my commandments with thee; So that thou incline thine ear unto wisdom, and apply thine heart to understanding . . . Then shalt thou understand righteousness, and judgment, and equity; yea, every good path.

Proverbs 2:1, 2, 9

39

Birthdays

Some families make a big thing out of birthdays, inviting everyone they can think of to celebrate (and bring presents). At some ages that's appropriate; at others it's silly.

Our one-year-olds tried to sleep through their first birthday parties, which were held in the evening at the convenience of the concerned adults. Aunts, uncles, parents, and grandparents sat around glumly, hoping the birthday boy would wake up for his cake and ice cream. When he didn't, we eventually woke him up and sat him in front of his cake. He made the obligatory mess of himself with the frosting and cried until he was allowed to escape the adult madness and go back to sleep.

At two years things went a little better. He enjoyed the wrapping paper and the boxes tremendously, ate a healthy serving of cake and ice cream, then spent the rest of the party defending his new toys from his neighborhood friends.

A three-year-old's party is an excuse for other mothers to check out your house while keeping an eagle eye on their children. Six three-year-olds sitting at a birthday table require one mother hovering behind each chair, mopping up the spilled soda, and saying things like "Suzie isn't allowed chocolate. Is there another cake?"

Birthdays   103

Four-year-olds couldn't care less about the cake and ice cream, but they get paranoid about their "goodie bags." Count out the candies carefully this year. Be sure each and every noisemaker works. Give everyone who plays any organized game a prize, no matter who wins. Make your husband blow up twice as many balloons as there are children.

By the time they're five you will realize the wisdom of having your children born during the warm-weather months. No one wants to have twenty-five kindergarten children for an indoor party. By now everyone is bored to tears with playing Pin the Tail on the Donkey, singing "Happy Birthday," and eating melted ice cream. Parties have become excuses for belching contests, violent, uncontrolled games of tag, and the destruction of brand-new toys.

Sometimes the parents get out of hand. We never hired a pony, clown, or magician for a party, despite peer pressure. Who needs an extra person around? Besides, they only put off the bedlam for about ten minutes. Not being martyrs, we never took a nursery-school class to a movie, a bowling alley, or a fast-food restaurant. Our kids made do with old-fashioned birthday parties until they hit the age of eight. That one year they could have whatever kind of party they wanted, with as many guests as they could gather, because that was *it* for birthday parties at our house.

Birthday parties can be nice or terrible, from an adult's point of view, but for the children involved they're always special, and for that reason worth the trouble to us.

However we choose to celebrate this day, Lord, help us remember we do it to make our child feel special and to let him

From Training Pants to Training Wheels

know how happy we are to have him as our child. Don't let the noise and gifts distract us from the true and lasting importance of this day.

And thou shalt rejoice in thy feast. . . .
Deuteronomy 16:14

40

Axioms:
Four to Five Years

No toy box is ever big enough.

No toys are ever in the toy box.

If you cook something new for dinner, no child over three will eat it.

No child ever asks questions you can answer. If you think you can, his teacher had a better answer.

Sweaters are for sissies.

It doesn't matter who "started it." Your job is to stop it.

A four-year-old who gives himself a bath comes out looking like a prune.

Never tell a four-year-old girl who dressed herself that the checked pants don't go with the print shirt.

41

If you have a four-year-old, you spend a lot of time in strange bathrooms. The four-year-old has mastered his bodily functions and *needs* to go to the bathroom everywhere. The more outlandish the place, the better.

I've climbed through supermarket stockrooms and up rickety stairs to bathrooms that never knew disinfectant. I've dashed down airline terminal corridors in high heels muttering, "Hold on. We'll find one." I've spent entire flights locked out of airplane rest rooms (you can't fit in), wondering what button my child was pushing in there.

It's always a good idea to wonder what a four-year-old is doing when he is beyond your reach, because whatever you can think of (and more), he will do. A four-year-old is off the wall most of the year.

He's happy, though. He's totally sure of himself and confident he can handle anything (except putting his pants back on). He doesn't walk, he *swaggers*. He boasts, and he scratches where it itches, in public. (This applies equally to boys and girls.)

A four-year-old doesn't have a lot of friends, because he

108   From Training Pants to Training Wheels

hits, bites, and gouges. His favorite words are "Make me." When you do make him, he will burst into self-righteous tears.

Most four-year-olds run away from home, causing their parents great worry, which was the purpose of the exercise. You've shackled a free spirit once too often and you will pay. My kids never officially ran away; they went to a neighborhood friend's house and refused to leave. Once the mother caught on, she would call and we would work out a strategy that involved her being stricter with him than I ever was. In an hour or less my child would return to the lesser evil, me.

Four-year-olds are impossible to eat with. They gulp down selected parts of their dinners and refuse to touch the rest. They kick chair legs, tip chairs back until they fall over, and leave the table four times to go to the bathroom. If you insist they clean their plates before leaving the table, you will be there for a long time. Our first son used the bathroom ruse to "eat" his peas. Our daughter buried the peas under her leftover mashed potatoes. Our second son fed them to the dog one at a time. After a while you let them get away with it because they wear you down.

It's hard not to like a four-year-old, despite his faults. How can you dislike someone who is absolutely, positively sure he can fly? All you can do is admire his spunk and keep him off the roof until he learns better!

Lord, this child does make me glad, so many times a day, and I thank You for that joy. More importantly, I thank You for his happiness, his unbounded confidence in a world that delights in confounding the confident. I wish he could always be so sure of himself, but I know that can't be. At least help him keep the joy, Lord, forever in his life.

Thy father and thy mother shall be glad, and she that bare thee shall rejoice.

Proverbs 23:25

42

Partly Cloudy

I don't know any mother of a four-year-old who doesn't listen to the morning weather forecast with trepidation. Here in the Northeast we get far too many days of rain and snow, and even more are "partly cloudy." A four-year-old needs *lots* of sun so he can play outside in his indoor clothes and give his mother no hassles about jackets, sweaters, or boots. Better yet, it should be warm enough so he will enjoy being hosed down before he comes back in the house!

I could deal with a rain-drenched day. I resigned myself to a day of indoor racket and fistfights, made lots of chocolate chip cookies, and checked *TV Guide* for the movies no one under twenty-one should watch, let alone

From Training Pants to Training Wheels

a roomful of four-year-olds. Two rainy days in row meant I had to take the modeling clay out of hiding and let them have it. Three days, and we checked for G-rated matinees. Four days, and I made my husband stay home while I escaped to the mall!

A blizzard is a little better. Four-year-olds love playing in new snow. But it has to be really new. At four the greatest neighborhood sin is leaving footprints all over another four-year-old's trackless front yard. My kids would stand out there and defend their virgin snow with a vengeance. Then they would get down to digging snow forts and engaging in warfare with the neighbors until someone got it in the eye with an iceball and I sent everyone home.

The problem is with partly cloudy days. They call for a jacket in case of rain, and no jacket ever comes home with a four-year-old. It sits out by the swing set or in a neighbor's toy box until someone identifies and returns it. If a four-year-old comes home with a jacket, he probably wasn't wearing one when he went out.

Partly cloudy makes trips of any kind risky. You pack the neighborhood into the station wagon, truck them all to the playground, sort out all those jackets, and have to repack on a raindrop's notice. You take them out for fast food and have to eat in the car during a thunderstorm, dodging French fries and mopping catsup off the rearview mirror.

The problem is, four-year-olds only come in six-packs. You can't take just your own child somewhere; he needs his best friends with him. You may not have invited them, but there they will be, sitting politely in the wagon, all lined up, smiling at you. How can you break their little hearts?

The only safe thing to do is listen to the morning weather forecast and send your four-year-old to the neighbor's to play at 9:00 A.M. on partly cloudy days. Maybe she will take them all to the movies this time.

It must be hard to be an active, bursting-with-energy four-year-old penned in by the weather. I understand this, Lord, on a fine, sunny day. Remind me of it when I reach my boiling point on the next partly cloudy day.

And not only so, but we glory in tribulations also: knowing that tribulation worketh patience; And patience, experience; and experience, hope.

Romans 5:3, 4

43

"Play With Me"

Eventually you'll have to play with your child. Not that you haven't been playing with him in little spontaneous spurts all his life: horseback rides, "Daddy's gonna getcha," tickling contests, and so on.

From Training Pants to Training Wheels

But someday there will be nothing good on television, all the neighborhood preschoolers will be unavailable, and it will be pouring outside. Your child will present you with an unopened Candy Land box and beg your attention. Okay, you can handle this, right?

Candy Land (or Chutes and Ladders) is a simple game. You read the rules and explain them in detail, set the board up, and begin. Everything goes fine while everything goes fine for him. He moves according to color and does exactly as instructed. Then he loses a turn or, worse yet, has to go back to Plumpy's square (for the uninitiated, that's *way* back!).

Now you have a problem. Do you throw the game and let him win, or do you build character and insist he follow the rules? Most parents opt for character building the first time. Suddenly your son can't distinguish colors. If you're foolish enough to look away from the board, his marker will mysteriously move to a better space. He will begin to fidget; eventually he will either cry or decide he "hates this stupid game." No preschooler ever finishes a board game unless he wins. So much for character building.

Different parents react differently to this situation. Some cave in and let their children win; some pretend not to see; others just sit there and watch their child openly cheat. Those made of sterner stuff stick to the rules come what may. I suspect they like their games short and stormy. (I *know* they do. I was one of them.)

What about Go Fish? They cheat at that, too, but it's harder to detect and easier to ignore. But little hands have trouble controlling cards, and little minds can only tell a jack from a king half the time. Try any game you want, the results will be the same: A frustrated child and a furious parent will collide. This is quality time?

Go back to playing horsey with him. Chase him around the house until you can't catch your breath. Wrestle him until he cries uncle. Have a pillow fight. Preschoolers need their games to be physical, noisy, and, best of all, with no winners or losers!

Father, I don't think my child is going to be the world's next five-year-old chess champion. I hope that's okay with You, but neither of us has the patience for it. I think I'll let him play whatever he wants to play, and hope for now it's not a board game.

. . . but he that is of a merry heart hath a continual feast.

Proverbs 15:15

44 War

The average four-year-old is a charming person, outgoing, friendly, and self-confident. If you find yourself alone with one, the two of you can actually enjoy a meaningful conversation.

The trouble is, you rarely find one alone. The odds are good that there is also a two-year-old in your family by now. Which leads to war.

It's not always the fault of the four-year-old, either. Nothing is more aggravating to a child of four than a little brother of two. The four-year-old builds elaborate block castles; his brother knocks them down. The four-year-old "shoots" his brother; his brother refuses to fall down. The four-year-old spends an hour drawing a Mother's Day card; it takes his brother one second to scribble all over it with black crayon.

And when you break up the fight, who do you hug? Who gets the blame? Who gets told, "You're supposed to take care of your little brother?" It doesn't take the oldest child long to learn that life isn't always fair.

It doesn't pay to feel sorry for the four-year-old, though. If you were omniscient, you would see that half the time he strikes the first blow—and makes it a good one. Four-year-olds have learned to be sneaky, and they get in their licks before you even know there's a storm brewing.

This constant state of red alert lasts for years, so you may as well learn to live with it. Sometimes you can recognize the danger signals in time to arrange a truce; sometimes nothing short of a bloody nose will end the skirmish. One minute they will be cheerfully washing each other's backs in the tub. The next minute one of them will be involuntarily under water.

You have to learn to defend yourself during this time of life. You can't get drawn into who started it or what he did or who called who "poopy." At our house anyone caught fighting was guilty, regardless of the provocation. It worked out to be fair in the long run. My ultimate defense after a rainy day filled with howls of outrage was "Everyone into his *own* room!" After half an hour of isolation even your own brother begins to look good.

Just when you've given up hope of them ever liking each other, you will look outside and see a circle of children on your lawn, the telltale sign of a good fight. On closer inspection you will see the two-year-old sheltered behind his older brother, who is shaking his fist at another four-year-old and saying, "You can't hit my brother! Only *I* can hit my brother!" It's too bad he can't see the look of adoration on his brother's face just then, but you will see it and know there is hope.

> *The next time my children blow up at each other, Lord, help me keep my cool. It's my job to teach them better ways of interacting and disagreeing than hair pulling and hitting. But I have to be reasonable to be effective, so keep me calm and help me set a good example through my actions.*

Let all bitterness, and wrath, and anger, and clamour, and evil speaking, be put away from you, with all malice: And be ye kind one to another, tenderhearted, forgiving one another, even as God for Christ's sake hath forgiven you.

Ephesians 4:31, 32

45

It's time for a little brutal honesty. If I am making it seem that the preschool years were a snap, that I never once raised my voice in anger or swatted an obstreperous two-year-old, that's a long way from reality!

Ask my kids. Jim will tell you about the time I threw a half-peeled potato in his direction, only missing him by inches because I have good aim. He will also tell you that now that his arms are longer than mine, I have taken up kicking him in the shins in cases of extreme anger. Laura still turns pale when she hears me say the word *three*, because for years we would calmly count to three before clobbering any offender.

I was a walking time bomb for about ten years there. I never held a grudge, but my retribution was swift and physical, with none of that "Wait till your father gets home" stuff. I would swat whatever bottom I could catch.

On the other hand, Bill was the voice of reason. He would sit the offender down, explain why his behavior was unacceptable, then tell the child to go to his room and prepare to be spanked. I was always the one who ended up crying. It was too calculating—why didn't the dumb kid just run off and hide? Luckily, it took a lot to get Bill mad enough to spank.

I don't know which method was the most effective. I

suspect my hair-trigger approach kept them on their toes, but Bill's organized punishments had long-term results. Together, they kept chaos and fratricide out of the house.

Parents lose it now and then. Two brothers spitting peas at each other during dinner can tick you off. When they leave the table and grind the peas into the linoleum, you would be abnormal if you didn't do a little yelling. If they laugh when you tell them to clean up the peas, they deserve whatever they get.

It wasn't what they did or said that set me off but the look of defiance or the ring of disrespect. They could say almost anything to me, if they used the right tone of voice and said it with love. But that's an awfully fine line for a preschooler to grasp, so I counted to three before swatting a young one. That gave me time to cool down and him time to say he was sorry.

It's been years since we've had an organized spanking around here. I don't miss them in the least. For a few years they were necessary, but they did their work and let us progress to reasonable discussion, with only a few shin kicks now and then.

Do I believe in physical punishment? Bet your boots I do! But I don't believe in chastisement, terrorizing, or self-righteousness. Kids may need a swat on the fanny now and then, but they deserve as much respect from me as I demand from them. Even when I lose it.

Father, You correct me when I blow it, but You do it with love and gentleness. Help me to correct my children the same way, not with harshness or bitterness.

From Training Pants to Training Wheels

For whom the Lord loveth he correcteth; even as a father the son in whom he delighteth.

Proverbs 3:12

46 Family Vacations

There are only a few years in life when you can take and enjoy family vacations.

With babies in the family it's too much bother. By the time you pack up all the necessary equipment and load the car, your husband is not speaking to you and the baby has heat rash. Even if you stubbornly carry on, you're still going to be sterilizing bottles and changing diapers all week instead of working on your tan. Better to go to Grandma's and get a little rest.

A toddler in the family makes any vacation a game of chance. Will you be able to find him soft-boiled eggs when he's ready for lunch at 2:00 P.M.? Where do you dispose of a diaper in the Grand Canyon? Will the hotel supply English-speaking baby-sitters you can trust? Will your child let you leave the room when the sitter arrives?

By the time your toddler has turned into a decent

traveler, you probably have another baby (*see* preceding caveat). Back to Grandma's.

We only found four good vacation years—from the ages of four to eight years. At that age children are anxious to see new things, relatively easy to feed and keep occupied, and almost enjoyable to be with twenty-four hours a day. You can go almost anywhere with a child between four and eight. He's eager to learn surfing, fishing, boating, and chipmunk taming. He'll charm waitresses and tour guides with his developing appetite and constant questions. He will stay with the sitter and let you escape for a night out. Of course you will have to stop every hour to find him a bathroom or feed him, but he generally sleeps between stops.

Once your child reaches nine, vacations get dicey again. You have to go to some fabulously expensive and intensely amusing spot to keep him occupied and reasonable. Teenagers absolutely *detest* any type of family vacation. School vacation times are too crowded, and no two children ever have the same week off once one gets to high school.

So if your kids are all between the ages of four and eight, *now* is the time to dig into the savings account and begin building family memories. This chance doesn't pass your way again.

Father, remind me that there is no such thing as a perfect vacation. Even when we go away and leave the kids at home, things go wrong. Help us make all our vacations times for sharing and laughter, times to warm the years to come.

From Training Pants to Training Wheels

Then was our mouth filled with laughter, and our
tongue with singing: then said they among the heathen,
The Lord hath done great things for them.

Psalms 126:2

47

Sickness

Sick children are easy to spot because they're not
running. You become conscious of a sudden silence in the
house when you know very well the child is home, so you
go exploring. Has he finally succeeded in taking the video
player apart? Is he sitting quietly on the toilet, pulling the
new wallpaper off the wall?

You'll find him on the sofa, bleakly staring at a soap
opera, his face flushed and his nose running. Sick—again.

From the day a child enters nursery school until he hits
puberty, he will be sick once a month. Maybe a little less
in summer, when he's more motivated to stay well, but it
averages out over the year.

Before I panicked and called the pediatrician, I used to
ask the sick one to sniffle for me, working on the premise
that a good runny nose meant the sickness wasn't serious.
There were times when that wasn't accurate, but in most

cases a runny nose was a good sign. It meant two to three days of tissues and chicken soup.

A hot forehead and dry nose were more serious. It could be the start of a *real* illness or one that might not get any worse and clear up on its own in a day or two. My pediatrician used to say if the fever's gone in one day, don't call, but if it hangs around, make the appointment. That way, any rash that's due will appear before you arrive at the office.

No runny nose and no hot forehead means there is some reason he doesn't want to go to nursery school that day. Send him off on the bus, but stay home in case you're wrong and the nurse calls. Isn't getting called by the nurse fun? You can tell by her tone of voice if you have seriously endangered the health of every four-year-old in town or if your child is an excellent actor. She doesn't always think he's sick, either, but unlike you she can't take the chance.

There is not much to question with an upset stomach; he's either got it or he hasn't. While this can be serious in an infant, it's just a messy inconvenience in a child. How the child takes it makes all the difference. I had one who thought she was going to die every time she had an upset stomach. I'd just get her calmed down before she had to get up and start all over. My second child couldn't have cared less. He had the stomach of a surgeon and would go on playing cheerfully until the last minute before making his controlled (and maddeningly slow) dash for the bathroom.

You do have to deal with some serious illnesses along the way, and they're scary. Our stoic son harbored a strep throat without telling us until it turned into scarlet fever. Our daughter broke her leg and spent a lonely week in a hospital during a nurses' strike. The other son got run over by a bike and broke his collarbone.

Of course, I didn't believe my son had scarlet fever (the rash changes your mind fast), my daughter had broken her leg (she took every bruise so seriously), or my other son had broken that collarbone (he always walked funny). The hardest part of a *real* sickness is that you have to get over your guilt before they can get well.

Luckily, God made children tough. I've seen my kids bounce back from colds that would have put their father in bed for a week. An autographed cast becomes an object of envy for every other child in the neighborhood. Stitches are super excuses for hibernating in front of a TV set. And there isn't a nursery-school teacher in the world who will insist a child help pick up the room if he can prove he was in the hospital for a week!

Father, please believe I'm serious when I ask You to bless my pediatrician. I need that man! Give him the grace not to laugh when my child's "deadly serious" fever disappears between home and his office. Help him keep his patience when I call at 2:00 A.M. and ask what to do about that funny rash I can't quite explain over the phone. Give this good doctor health and a long, happy life.

Beloved, I wish above all things that thou mayest prosper and be in health. . . .

3 John 1:2

48
Handprints

I've changed my mind about handprints.

For twenty-plus years I waged war on them and lost. I had them all—jam prints on sliding glass doors, chocolate stains on doorjambs, bloody-nose handprints on the bathroom counter—plus others I didn't even *attempt* to identify.

We're not talking about the adorable baby handprints every parent puts in the new patio cement; those are planned for and treasured. We're talking about plain old dirt here.

Doorways of connecting rooms attract a lot of handprints, children being physically incapable of rounding a corner at full tilt without a slight wall-swing on the way. Even if you've just yelled at him about it and are sitting right there as he goes by, he'll still reach out his hand onto the corner as he passes.

And why do they insist on ignoring a perfectly serviceable banister to press their grubby hands on the wall all the way up or down the stairs? That seems the hard way to do it, but they must get some satisfaction from it.

I can understand handprints on wall switches, but the one-foot radius of dirt on all sides of the switch puzzles me. Are they really that inaccurate at finding the switch, or is there a corner wall-swing involved in entering a room and turning on the light?

Little toddlers on potty seats leave handprints on the top of the toilet-seat rim. Bigger boys leave them on the underside of the seat they never put down when they're done. Little girls and mothers complain a lot about little boys and fathers.

One year my husband had both a four-year-old and a car with leather seats. Bad timing. Even though no food, drink, or gum was allowed in the car, the top of the front seats still turned grey where his little hands hung on for dear life. Luckily another driver totalled the car before my husband totalled the four-year-old.

But I've changed my mind about handprints. There is one on our living-room ceiling that testifies to the fact that our youngest can now put his palms flat on the ceiling without standing on anything. A sliding glass door holds a tiny visiting baby's print at an improbable height—right where he came to when I held him up to show him a bright red cardinal in the snow. Once you begin to face the fact that your children are growing up and are about to leave home, some handprints become worth saving.

There is never any doubt that children live in our house, Father. Even when they're not home, their clutter and dirt is. Maybe it should bother me more than it does, but I don't have time to keep a sparkling house. I don't think I even want one. Remind me of that the next time I yell at a child with grubby hands.

Behold, thou desireth truth in the inward parts: and in the hidden part thou shalt make me to know wisdom.

Purge me with hyssop, and I shall be clean: wash me, and
I shall be whiter than snow.

Psalms 51:6, 7

49

Socks

A mother spends far too much time dealing with socks. One day some genius is going to invent cheap disposable socks and make a well-deserved fortune.

Tiny babies require tiny socks for those occasions when stretchy jumpsuits aren't appropriate—blizzards, for example. You buy ones with pink ruffles for girl babies and tiny stripes for boy babies. They fall off two minutes after you put them on. If they don't fall off, the baby pulls them off and eats them. If you buy the kind with elastic so they won't fall off, they make tiny indentations in your baby's legs and cause you to worry about the blue color of his ankles. Baby shoes don't control baby socks, although it's logical that they should. The socks just creep down and desert the baby's heel, sulking in a lump at the toes.

A preschooler's crew socks are more reliable. They don't stay up, but no one honestly cares, either. The main problem with crew socks is that they all look alike, especially inside out, which is the way they go into my washing machine. I don't know about you, but I have no intention of putting my hand inside anyone's sock and turning it right-side out *before* it's gone through at least one wash! They go in the way I find them, usually scrunched into an evil-looking ball on a bedroom floor.

When they come out of the dryer, half of them are still wet at the toes and have to go back for another toasting. Meanwhile I sort the survivors, turning them right-side out and searching for stripes that match. It takes a day to get them all folded together and back in the right drawers.

Even then, I always find at least two socks with no mates at the end of the day. It's tempting to feel sorry for an unmatched sock sitting all alone on top of someone's dresser. Don't. Socks are natural loners; they love being on their own and unusable.

If your children are four or five years old and it's summer, half of the unmatched socks aren't even yours. Sometimes you get lucky and turn up a whole pair of orphans that fit your child. Keep them; he has left plenty of replacements at the neighbors' houses. You can go crazy trying to remember which neighborhood mother bought her child purple stripes. Maybe you don't want to know.

You can look for a lost sock for a long time. There's a 25 percent chance it will show up with the next load of laundry, but there's only a 50 percent chance that you can now locate its original mate, which has probably been used to store toy soldiers. Another quarter of the time the original missing sock is floating loose in the wrong drawer, under a bed, behind the washer, or out by the swing set. Every three months I gather together all the unmatched socks and perform a random mating. At this point, two blue-striped socks go together, whether or not the stripes are the same width or shade of blue. I usually get away with it—kids don't care if their socks match perfectly.

One year I got clever and bought brand-name socks for my boys. The names were knit right into the top of the sock; how could I go wrong? Here's where the truly evil nature of socks is revealed. I'd frustrated them; they always matched. So one sock of each pair sacrificed itself and wore out or unraveled in its second week of life. You could almost hear the cheers coming out of the washing machine as another gave his life in the battle with Mother.

Yes, Lord, I know the problem is me, not the socks. But I haven't found the solution, so let me take it out on an inanimate object, not on my children. Things sometimes get out of control, despite my best efforts, but You understand that. You don't expect me to be perfect. Thank You for that.

It is better to dwell in the wilderness, than with a contentious and an angry woman.

Proverbs 21:19

50

Shoes

What is it about the nether regions of a child that drives a mother to distraction? Socks are fairly easy to understand—they're contentious and evil—and the best you can do with them is be nasty in return. But shoes give you another set of problems.

You spend an awful lot of time in shoe stores if you have three children. I was in there once a month on a rotating-child basis for at least five years of my life. At twenty-five dollars a pop, the sales staff became close family friends.

You start asking the pediatrician when to buy the baby his first set of shoes as soon as he is fairly mobile. He's walking pretty well by now, and the yard isn't all that clean, and you feel he needs a little protection down there. The pediatrician is older than you and more experienced, so he or she puts you off for a visit or two, but eventually you take yourself to the shoe store and ask for a pair of shoes for the baby. If you think the salesperson is smiling at you for no discernible reason, you're wrong!

Babies don't like shoes any more than they like socks, but they're pliable little animals and they get used to them. Your baby will fall down a lot more with shoes than without, and he'll learn to untie the laces years before he learns to tie them, but that's life. In a month or so he will be used to wearing shoes, you will feel better about being

Shoes   129 a competent mother, and he will outgrow the shoes—every month for the next two years at twenty-five dollars a pop.

It doesn't take you long to get bored with those white little shoes that need polishing every other day, so you start looking for something different. In my day that meant brown oxfords. All they needed to make them look like real people was a briefcase and a pair of pants that would stay up five minutes. Back then, little children weren't allowed sneakers until they hit three or four. Now I see brand-name sneakers are available in sizes so tiny they must be worn by newborns—they're adorable!

Toddlers require more than one set of shoes since one set is always muddy or wet. This is the point at which I began buying sneakers, *real* sneakers, the kind you can throw into the washer and dryer and take out in one piece. No leather, no plastic, just good, heavy canvas that could take anything a toddler could dish out. I made the mistake of buying "cute" sneakers one time, the kind where the sole comes up and covers the toe. It took my son three days to wear that sole right off his toe. I had forgotten that he used his toes to brake with when riding his trike.

I went to the wedding of my daughter's best friend the other day. My daughter has known the groom's family for years, but the groom's father always had the feeling he knew Laura from somewhere before—long before. It wasn't until he saw me in the reception line that it dawned on him. He was the smiling shoe salesman I'd been seeing on a monthly basis for all those years!

Lord, am I trying to rush my child's growing up? Does it make him feel better to wear designer sneakers or to go barefoot in the

grass? Does my daughter want shiny Mary Janes, or do I? Help
me keep my priorities straight so I will do what's right for them,
not what I want for them.

The way of a fool is right in his own eyes: but he that
hearkeneth unto counsel is wise.

Proverbs 12:15

51

In Stitches

If you have a four-year-old, you know where your Blue
Cross card is at all times. It's in your purse, snuggled next
to the butterfly bandages above the antiseptic swabs.

By the time your child reaches four, you're an expert at
first aid. The boo-boo of the first two years has turned into
a gaping gash that requires at least four stitches. Your
stomach has matured, too. Head wounds that would have
made you retch two years ago are nothing special now.
You've learned that no bodily part bleeds as profusely,
and suffers as little damage, as the head.

By four, most children are beginning to bear some
resemblance to Frankenstein: more stitches than skin.

They wear them like medals of honor, recounting the story behind each stitch to any adult who will listen. If Grandma turns green, so much the better.

You see, a four-year-old knows he's invincible. The worse that can happen to him is a trip to the emergency room and a new line of stitches, and by now he knows they don't hurt very much. Most four-year-olds haven't broken any bones yet, and the concept of death hasn't sunken in. So he can climb out his bedroom window, swing over to the tree, and scamper to the ground without a qualm. If he falls, he'll get stitches. Big deal.

It's not a good year for mothers, who are physically incapable of being with their children twenty-four hours a day. The nursery-school nurse and I developed a standard conversation that year.

"Hi, Mrs. Sortor. It's Joan again."

"Hi. Stitches?"

"Two or three."

"Be right there."

"I'll call your pediatrician and tell him you're on the way."

I'd arrive to find my son sitting in the office eating a "stitches lollipop," pressing a sterile dressing to whatever part of him was leaking. The school's dog would be pressed against him, offering comfort. A few sniffles for effect, a hug to comfort me, and he'd bound out the door calling, "See you tomorrow!"

And how did I take all this blood and gore? Surprisingly well. I had worked in a hospital emergency room and seen far worse, so I could keep my cool. I could even help other mothers decide between a Band-Aid and a call for the ambulance. I could joke with the nurses and doctors and convince my child he was going to be fine, once we patched him up and hosed him down.

But inside there's a little place behind the stomach that curls up tight and sends shivers up the spine of any mother with a bleeding child. I know that spot well.

Lord, I know You'll take care of my child this year. You always do. But could I ask You to help me, too? Keep me from the panic that delays needed help and teaches my child to be too fearful. On the other hand, don't let me shrug off injuries that need professional help. It's a fine line to walk, but with Your help, I know we'll make it.

For I will restore health unto thee, and I will heal thee of thy wounds, saith the Lord. . . .

Jeremiah 30:17

52

Axioms:
Five to Six Years

All five-year-olds want to ride their bikes to school like the big kids, but training wheels aren't cool.

No child is tired enough for a nap after kindergarten. He just lies on the floor and rests his eyes a lot.

Jeans don't quite stay up by themselves, but bib overalls are an embarrassment.

No child with a cold will take his own tissues to school. All teachers have a big box of them on their desks.

Once a class mother, always a class mother.

The only day your son will wear a designer shirt and real slacks to school is on opening day.

No child willingly wears boots to school, no matter how deep the snowdrifts on the playground are.

53

Facts

It didn't take our kids long to learn that if they wanted a quick answer, they should come to me. If they wanted to know everything there was to know about a subject, they should ask their father at the dinner table.

A child would come running in from a game of tag to ask me what the big black bird in the tree was. I'd look, say "crow," and that would be that. Their father, on the other hand, would tell them where crows live, how long they live, what they eat, and the rather remarkable fact that crows can count up to five hunters in a field, but not the sixth one.

I always thought he went on a bit too long. After the first few minutes, my eyes would glaze over and I'd begin to try and stop him, figuring the kids were as bored as I was. I doubted that a five-year-old needed or wanted to understand the theories behind an inclined plane; he just wanted a ramp to ride his bicycle off, like Evel Knievel.

But they kept asking questions, and he kept the torrent of facts coming, night after night, year after year. The rocket propulsion lecture was a big hit with the boys;

Laura liked learning how eyes and other lenses work. I thought photosynthesis boggled their little minds until I saw one of them looking in wonder at the underside of a leaf.

It got to be a family joke. The first one to say, "Dad, how does ——— work?" would be greeted with catcalls and cries of "Oh, no! Another lecture!" But no one left the table.

One day Jim came home from kindergarten with a smirk on his face. When we asked him why he was so pleased with himself, he told us he had just explained to his classmates and his teacher that crows can count to five. He was amazed that they didn't know that. Didn't they have fathers? I figured by the time they got to photosynthesis in school he was going to be in pretty good shape.

Each parent has his own way of teaching and relating to his children, and it's best for the other to stay out of the way. It's also amazing how much a child retains when he's taught out of love.

Father, give me the grace to stand back and not get in the way of my husband when he's working with our children. I may think he's going about it the wrong way, but I'm more than willing to admit I could be wrong. Even in this day and age, fathers often do know best.

Furthermore we have had fathers of our flesh which corrected us, and we gave them reverence. . . .

Hebrews 12:9

54 Readiness Testing

Your child has been a responsible nursery-school student for two years now. He doesn't cry when the bus picks him up (or when it drops him off). He's learned how to deal with bullies and wimps, knows all his letters, and can count to ten without messing up seven, eight, and nine. It's time for kindergarten!

Maybe. It all depends on whether or not his birthdate is before your school system's cutoff date. In our town the cutoff date was September 30, which left our third child, born October 12, out in the cold for another year.

By this time I was an experienced school parent, though; I knew he could still get in if he passed the readiness test. So I cleaned out his ears, found his one pair of jeans without holes in the knees, and turned him over for testing.

He failed. A committee of educators and psychologists decided he wasn't mature enough for kindergarten. I knew they were wrong, but I was left to explain to my totally ready son why he was going back to nursery school for a postgraduate degree.

In the long run I'm glad he failed. He's been the oldest, biggest boy in his class ever since. In many ways he's more mature than his classmates. It worked out okay. But sometimes I think that rejection still bothers him and colors his relationship with both teachers and administrators. Little boys hold mature grudges!

I can't protect my child from the world's emotional blows anymore, Lord. Maybe I shouldn't even try. He has to learn to cope with teasing, name calling, and more subtle swats to his tender ego. All I can do is assure him he is loved, no matter what, and valuable to me and You. I hope it's enough.

For God hath not given us the spirit of fear; but of power, and of love, and of a sound mind.

2 Timothy 1:7

55

Graduation

Nursery-school graduation is the most entertaining ceremony you'll ever giggle your way through. As children get older, their graduations become more solemn, until by the time they pick up their college diplomas, rigor mortis has set in. I guess they figure you've spent $60,000 for that diploma so you should take it seriously.

There is no such pretense in nursery school. The children march up front with their mortarboards on at all angles, behaving like perfect ladies and gentlemen for exactly two minutes. They sing a cute song with gusto until one of them gets the giggles and it spreads like chicken pox through the ranks, leaving two serious little blonde girls to belt it out alone while the rest of the class hoots it up.

The director of the school then makes a little speech thanking you for your support and assuring you your child—he's the one who has just discovered a mortarboard has all the properties of a Frisbee—is prepared for kindergarten. The little dark-haired girl next to your son pokes him in the ribs as he tosses his hat to someone in the back row, throwing off his aim just enough so the hat lands in the fish tank. By the time the school dog retrieves it to your son, they've mercifully dimmed the lights to show slides.

The slides are wonderful. There's their visit to the zoo, where your son fed his baseball cap to a hungry goat. There they all are on the fire engine, fighting to ring the bell. There's naptime, all of them lined up on their little rugs, just waiting for the photographer to leave so they can get back to whispering insults to one another.

It's obvious that something is going on while you're looking at the slides. You hear lots of scuffling around, vague mutterings, teachers saying "Shh!" and the yelp of the dog who's obviously been stepped on once too often. It sounds too much like your house ten minutes after the last bedtime warning, and you know an adult had better get in there soon.

The sudden glare of the lights freezes everyone in a

From Training Pants to Training Wheels

tableau of mayhem. There are children under chairs, on top of chairs, with chairs in their hands, but not one is sitting on his chair. With her best "Aren't they sweet?" smile, the director announces there will be a short break for cookies and juice before the awards and diplomas are presented.

Order restored through the administration of cookies, you find that every child in the class has won an award. Your son has been named Class Clown, a title he will invariably live up to through the next seventeen years of schooling. He hits his best friend over the head with his award as he follows you out the door.

"Good-bye, dummy!"

"So long, drip!"

These are the things memories are made of.

Lord, sometimes my child embarrasses me in public, and I often have a hard time not laughing along with him. I'm glad he doesn't take himself too seriously. Thank You for giving him all that joy and spontaneity in his life.

Blessed is the people that know the joyful sound: they shall walk, O Lord, in the light of thy countenance.

Psalms 89:15

56

Cash or Charge?

Everyone knows having children is an expensive hobby. You would be better off financially keeping horses out back. No horse ever wanted to go to Dartmouth, and their shoes are dirt cheap. But people keep on having children, even though the cost of each is now into six figures.

The obvious costs are bad enough, but it's the hidden costs that do you in. For example, sofas. It takes years for a child's legs to grow long enough so he can sit on a sofa without his dirty shoes on the cushions. If you tell him to take his shoes off, he'll spill the orange soda he's holding. Sofas are great places to put down a baby (you hem him in with pillows and tickle his tummy while you watch TV together), but babies spit up all over sofas. Three-year-olds color happily in coloring books while sitting on sofas, but tend to slip out of the lines and leave colored marker streaks on the upholstery. We've had three sofas since we've been parents, one for each child.

Washing machines cost money, too. Every repairman in the county—and I know them all personally—has told me the average life of a washer is five to seven years, but they must be talking about those owned by senior citizens. Our washer runs at least two hours a day, longer on weekends or hot summer days. They die on us every two years and five months, like clockwork.

From Training Pants to Training Wheels

Refrigerators last longer; it's air conditioning the kitchen with them that's expensive. Ever timed how many minutes a day a five-year-old spends in front of an open refrigerator? What is he doing, waiting for something in there to move? Nothing but leftover pot roast stays in there long enough to learn how to move. (Does anyone eat leftover pot roast? It seems like leftovers the first time I serve it.)

Swing sets are another hidden expense. We went through two department-store swing sets, at nearly a hundred dollars each, before we got smart. One summer of hard use and the seats on the glider loosened up and bucked children headfirst into the dirt. One winter enough rust grew on the pipes to require a neighborhood tetanus clinic. We finally bought a swing set from a school-supply company. It only has two swings—no slides, no gliders, no ladders—and it's made of two-inch galvanized steel pipe, not pie tins. It's lasted over fifteen years.

Then there's the cost of the grass. My husband always had visions of his children romping on a perfect lawn—no weeds, no bugs, no little bare patches, just gorgeous turf. That was his hang-up, and he paid for it with hours of work, tons of fertilizer, and enough seed to fatten every starling in the county. The kids romped on it, all right. They also stomped on it, wore paths in it, ate it, pulled it up by the roots, and packed it down. He won't get his perfect lawn until they all grow up and leave home, and then it will be too empty to enjoy.

Children are expensive playthings, all right, but what better use do we have for our money? They don't make a stereo that can call me Mommy in the right tone of voice. No car feels as comfortable to me as a sleepy four-year-old's hugs. No boat is as thrilling as helping a baby learn to talk. Besides, I prefer long-term investments.

Father, how can we never have enough money but always find enough for what we really need? Maybe the line between wanting and needing becomes a little clearer when we have children to feed and clothe. Thank You for providing us with enough for the necessities and giving us hope for the things we'd just like to have.

. . . provide yourselves bags which wax not old, a treasure in the heavens that faileth not, where no thief approacheth, neither moth corrupteth. For where your treasure is, there will your heart be also.

Luke 12:33, 34

57

Five

Society has decided to accept your baby and he's enrolled in kindergarten. As opening day approaches, you both have mixed emotions. He's still shy and a bit over-whelmed by his widening world, but, on the other hand, he's eager to get out there and take a shot at it. If he has older brothers or sisters, they will have filled him in on school. He will want notebooks and book covers and pencils and (the greatest gift of all) real ballpoint pens, the kind you never let him have because he scribbles indiscriminately now and then.

Even though he may have been in nursery school for a year or two, you're a little worried, too. After all, you *paid* the nursery school to be nice to him; kindergarten is free. We all worry about anything that's free, don't we?

It's always sunny on the first day of school, which is handy because you'll be standing out there by that red door for some time. You will be early because your five-year-old got up at the crack of dawn; now he's dressed, brushed, scrubbed, and shiny in his new school clothes. There will be a large crowd by the kindergarten door: children in various stages of dismay or giddiness, mothers holding little hands and stifling yawns, stray dogs, older children pushing and shoving their sullen way through the crowd to their own doors—in short, it's a zoo!

In the midst of this madness a few heads rise above the crowd. These few calm, happy, wide-awake people—the kindergarten teachers—now make their way through the crowd, greet shiny little faces, and gather hangers-on as they go (most of those attaching themselves to the teachers will be little girls).

You find yourself looking at other parents. What's the proper attitude on this occasion? Do you hang onto your child's hand for mutual support? You can tell he's scared by all the noise and pushing, but you don't want him to know you're scared, too. If you don't take his hand, will he wander off and get hopelessly lost? Will he think you're abandoning him in all the confusion? It's hard to straighten it all out in your mind when you haven't even had a cup of coffee.

I used to hold their hands until they showed me I didn't have to; it comforted me, and I have the sneaky feeling that I was the one who needed comforting the most.

Eventually those smiling faces will begin to line up the children in some order. Some will go into line alone; others will have their mothers hanging on like tall append-ages. A bell will ring, the red door will open, and the line will surge into the building. Clinging mothers will be detached at the door (there are always a few who hang on for dear life and actually get inside, but it's in poor taste). In a matter of minutes the door will close, leaving a sad collection of parents out on the blacktop.

Now what do you do? A few experienced mothers will turn away and stride purposefully to their waiting cars. A few more will swallow hard, look back once, and wander off slowly. Most aren't quite ready to let go; they surge like enraged mother elephants to the kindergarten windows, pressing their noses to the panes, waving, smiling, crying, and totally embarrassing their children. I did that once. My child was too busy fighting for a choice coat hook to even look at me. From then on I just went back to my car and cried for five minutes.

You eventually have to go home alone and face the fact that your child is now at the mercy of the system. It's a relief. It's a tragedy. You've spent years loving, training, guiding, and praying for that child. You were his world, and you made that world safe for him. But now it's out of your hands and strangers will have him for several hours a day. Will what they teach him agree with your beliefs? There's no guarantee of that. Will they know that he can't unbutton the top button of his new coat? It will be obvious when he sits down with his coat on. Will they love him the way you do? Of course not.

It takes several hours to work your way through all these questions, and the next thing you know, you're back in your car. Once more, you stand outside the red door with the other anxious parents, waiting to see what has happened to your child in those few hours. The door opens, a mob of yelling children appears, and suddenly you feel your hand grasped tightly. He may be smiling, crying, pulling, laughing, it doesn't matter. He has come back to *you*.

Dear Lord, I gave up my child to the system today. Because I'm much older and wiser than he, it scared me. Remind me that I'm still his teacher, though. They may teach him to read and write, but I have to watch over the content of his reading and writing. While his mind may be theirs for a few hours a day, his soul is still my responsibility, so give me Your guidance as together we educate my child to take his place in Your world.

Train up a child in the way he should go: and when he is old, he will not depart from it.

Proverbs 22:6

58

Friends

Once he's in school, friends become important to a child. Not that he hasn't had playmates before; all children coalesce in groups. The difference is that now he chooses his friends, not you.

He's outgrown the limited number of children in the neighborhood, but kindergarten provides an unending supply of new children he wants to play with. His former best friend, who saw him through tricycle riding and castle building, no longer meets his requirements. Everyone he wants to play with now lives on the other side of town. Every day you will have to drive him to someone's house, have someone driven to your house, or live with a bored five-year-old—a fate to be avoided at all cost!

You do meet a lot of other parents during this stage of life. You meet them on the phone: "Hi, this is Steve's mother. Steve would like to know if Mike can come over and play this afternoon." Although you talk to these parents every day, they don't have names. They're "John's mother" or "Peter's father" or "David's baby-sitter." Soon you will learn a little more about them and they become "Peter's father, who never picks him up on time," or "John's mother, who doesn't let him snack between meals." Sometimes you wonder how you're pegged in the minds of other parents. Don't let yourself think about it, it's only your reputation.

If you're one of those people who genuinely loves children (this can't be faked, they *know*), and if you don't work outside the home, in about one month everyone will be playing at your house. You get to stop the games of "Let's see who can jump from the highest step without breaking anything." You get to decide whether Tommy was really peeking when he was it or had something in his eye, as he so loudly claims. You sort out who can have what for a snack and who has to sit there and watch like the puppy. You keep the cupboard stocked with Band-Aids and kiss the scraped elbows, deciding when to call the pediatrician or visit the emergency room. You decide what you will and will not see in the course of play. There could be a whole book on this skill alone.

But it's worth it, because all this playing is doing something good for your child. He's learning how to share. He cooperates with others a little more. He's getting his act together and beginning to look like a responsible person—if you can call anyone who cheats at Candy Land responsible.

Just when you have all his friends straightened out and have memorized all their individual requirements, he hates every one of them. Don't try to figure out why. There's only childlike logic behind it, and mothers don't understand that. Accept that you now have to deal with "Joe's mother" and "Dan's father" on the phone.

Hint: Never invite two children over; invite one or three. For some reason children only get along when there is an even number in the house. If you have three, two will invariably gang up on the third, leaving you to comfort the outcast and necessitating a serious discussion with your child when they all go home. These discussions never do a bit of good, but they are obligatory.

At this stage of life girls are as noisy as boys. They also have a few unpleasant traits boys don't have. Little girls can be witches. They can be catty and cruel, carry big grudges, and spread kindergarten rumors. Boys, on the other hand, will just sock an offender and resume the friendship as soon as the swelling goes down.

Friends are wonderful; they just require certain adjustments to your life-style. All in all, a house swarming with unrelated children is a happy one.

Lord, I never knew this town harbored so many five-year-olds! They come out of the woodwork on a rainy day, and most of them aren't too sure of their telephone numbers when I desperately need them. But they do make a joyful noise around this house, and I'm glad they want to be here.

Make a joyful noise unto the Lord, all ye lands.

Psalms 100:1

From Training Pants to Training Wheels

59

Lessons

Suddenly you have a little student in the house. He's become competent at some pretty complex tasks, such as taking care of his own personal needs, making friends, and conning his kindergarten teacher. Now he wants to move on to the more important things, like learning to ride a two-wheeler without training wheels.

Teaching a child to ride a bike should be a job for his father, since it involves brute force, running, and a good set of lungs. But fathers are too macho in their teaching techniques. My husband's idea of teaching involved putting a child on the bike, giving him a good push down the driveway, and yelling, "Pedal!" After two or three good falls, our children would decide their father was trying to kill them and quit in a huff. Once the bruises healed, I'd take them back to the driveway and teach them the right way, which involves hanging on to the back of the seat and running downhill for all you're worth while the kid tries to get his feet onto the pedals. A few skinned knees later, he learns.

They also learn to swim about now. If you've just watched your husband try to teach his son how to ride a bike, you may decide to send the child to a *real* swimming teacher. It's hard to escape visions of Daddy letting go and yelling, "Swim!"

Lessons   151

Readiness for swimming lessons depends not only on the child's eagerness to learn, but also on his height. He can't hear the swimming instructor well enough when his head is underwater at the shallow end. We were fortunate to have a pool in our yard, so our children learned to swim early in self-defense. I can still see our middle child's wide eyes peering up at me from the shallow end the day he slipped off the lowest step. We took him off to the local swimming instructor who whipped him into shape and had him doing laps in less than a week. Motivation is wonderful stuff.

Soon your child will begin a continuously changing series of lessons. Your son will want to take judo, your daughter will beg for piano lessons, your preschooler will get into the act with acrobatics. Parents never learn. They're so happy to see their children interested in something besides television that they immediately agree to any requests for lessons that are within their budgets. They'll go so far as to rent guitars and buy pianos for their children if it will turn the little animals into civilized human beings!

But lessons don't do that. Lessons keep you shivering in your car all winter, waiting for them to end. Lessons require that you attend recitals and demonstrations, where you can plainly see your child has made absolutely no progress. Lessons mean practice; you have one more thing to hound your child about.

Equally frustrating is that no second child ever wants to take the same lessons his older brother or sister took, so that new piano will sit unused forever. None of my children ever lasted a year at any given lesson. As soon as things began to get hard and they were required to learn

From Training Pants to Training Wheels

something, it was over. I know there are children who do keep up their lessons for years and develop into talented cello players, but face it, the odds against that happening with your child are astronomical.

The nice thing about parents is that we keep on believing in our children, despite all the evidence.

Father, where did this complex little person come from? Sometimes I can almost see him being pulled apart by all the demands on him. His teacher wants this, his friends that, and we expect him to act his age. Help me realize that's exactly what he is doing. He's only five, and I ask too much of him some days.

Hear, O my son, and receive my sayings; and the years of thy life shall be many. . . . Take fast hold of instruction; let her not go: keep her; for she is thy life.

Proverbs 4:10, 13

60 Kindergarten

Kindergarten is just nursery school with rules added, as far as parents are concerned. The papers your child brings home don't look different, except that the school's copying machine is a little muddier than the one at the nursery school. Nothing magical happens, and there are no sudden changes to worry you.

But something is happening. Before, your son could spend the day in the sand pile if he wanted to. If he was interested in learning his letters, someone would teach them to him; if not, no one pushed him. Now his freedom is slowly and gently being restricted. He's expected to work with the group, not off in the corner by himself. Most of the time this only causes minor rebellions you won't even hear about. There aren't too many children who decide they hate school this year.

But you'll notice some changes when he comes home. Your four-year-old had totally outgrown naps; your five-year-old will likely fall asleep on the floor a half hour after getting home. If he doesn't you might wish he would, because he's tired and cranky and he doesn't want any suggestions from you, thank you!

When he regains consciousness, he's going to be filled with manic energy, flitting from one activity to another like a man possessed. He's going to fight with his friends, growl at the dog, and eat anything you will allow. In a few hours he'll regain control and turn back into the sweet, cooperative child you were beginning to miss.

Kindergarten simply overloads them at first. Too much is new, too much is being asked of them, even in the best-run kindergarten in the world. Luckily, children adapt rapidly. In a few weeks he'll drop his nap again and play happily with his friends. He won't be afraid of the first graders who bully him on the playground. The bells won't make him jump out of his seat. He'll settle down and tell you Mrs. Brown knows a *lot* more than you.

Good. Let Mrs. Brown handle all those questions no one in the world knows the answers to! You've suddenly got your hands full, anyway. It seems your son has discovered he has the power to volunteer you. They can't go to the police station without another mother? You're a mother. They need three dozen cupcakes by 8:30 A.M. tomorrow? He's sure you know how to make cupcakes and will be able to find a way to transport thirty-six slippery cupcakes in the car without smudging the frosting. Class mother? Why not?

Stop him right there! Class mothers go on *all* the trips the class takes. Class mothers get up in the darkness of 6:00 A.M. on snow days and call every other mother in the class to say there's no school. It's wonderful that he feels so involved with his class, so responsible for their fun, but enough is enough!

By winter he will be bringing home papers that are definitely in the schoolwork category. They'll have clowns and seals and balloons on them, but you'll realize he's learning the properties of numbers and printing short words on funny-looking paper. Something is going on inside there.

Something is changing in his play, too. It's getting more complex, more cooperative, more imaginative. By the time kindergarten is over, your baby is gone. He's been replaced by a confident little individual who can't wait to get out there and make his mark as one of the "big kids."

It's amazing how they change in one short year, Lord. He's learned so much about life this year that I can't call him my baby anymore; now he's a full-fledged child. Thank You for staying with him and helping him grow.

When I was a child, I spake as a child, I understood as a child, I thought as a child: but when I became a man, I put away childish things.

1 Corinthians 13:11

61

Babyhood's End

Congratulations, you've just delivered a child!

In six short years you've taken a helpless, totally dependent baby and taught him how to survive. He can now eat on his own, take care of his bodily functions, relate to others of his species, walk, run, talk, and tell a funny joke. He's no longer a dependent animal. He's a person, comfortable and secure in his world, thanks to you.

Oh, the job is far from done, but most of what follows he will do on his own or with the help of others with specialized training. There will be many teachers in his life from now on, building on the base you've provided. There's so much for him to learn that you welcome the help.

Your job has changed, though. You have spent years being the whole world to your child. All love, warmth, security, and joy either came from you or was reflected in your eyes. In a real sense, you were his god.

From Training Pants to Training Wheels

Now you're going to be demoted to plain old Mom and Dad, because he is going out into a wider world than he has ever known. He's going to discover there are people out there smarter than you. He's going to find friends he would rather be with than you. He's going to find God for himself and know you aren't Him.

It's a bit like doing wood sculpture. Up to now you've been working with the saw and chisel, roughing out the form of the design, separating it from the extraneous wood that you don't want in the final product. Now the design is formed, it's there for everyone to see, but it's still rough around the edges. It needs fine sandpaper to take a little off there, round that curve, and straighten that line. That's what you will be doing for the next few years: perfecting your work of art, making it the best you can.

Eventually, like Pinocchio, your piece of art will consider himself done, shake off your sawdust, and walk off into the sunset without you. What more could you possibly wish for him?